Social capital

An Introduction to Managing Networks

Kenneth W. Koput

University of Arizona, USA

Edward Elgar
Cheltenham, UK • Northampton, MA, USA

Published by
Edward Elgar Publishing Limited
The Lypiatts
15 Lansdown Road
Cheltenham
Glos GL50 2JA
UK

Edward Elgar Publishing, Inc.
William Pratt House
9 Dewey Court
Northampton
Massachusetts 01060
USA

Paperback edition 2011

A catalogue record for this book
is available from the British Library

Library of Congress Control Number: 2009941278

MIX
Paper from
responsible sources
FSC
www.fsc.org   FSC® C018575

ISBN 978 1 84980 099 0 (cased)
ISBN 978 1 78100 156 1 (paperback)

Typeset by Servis Filmsetting Ltd, Stockport, Cheshire
Printed and bound in Great Britain by Marston Book Services Limited, Didcot

Contents

Foreword

This book contains a course in social capital, covering both substantive and analytic material. Part I introduces basic theory, concepts and terminology and applies them to business and human resource management. Part II covers considerations in obtaining relational data and preparing the data for analysis on the computer. Part III presents the methods for social network analysis.

Social network analysis was until recently a relatively unknown branch of sociology and anthropology. The development of menu-driven computer software packages has opened up access for business and human resource managers, among others. Two of the more popular software packages are UCINET and Pajek. The software and tutorials are easy to obtain on the internet.

Yet the tools themselves are of little value without an understanding of concepts that can relate the computed measures to relevant applications. In this text, the focus is foremost on gaining such an understanding. Social capital provides a framework for relating the abstract world of graph theory, which underlies network analysis, to the concrete world of human behavior.

PART I

THEORY AND APPLICATIONS

This part introduces basic theory, concepts and terminology and applies them to business and human resource management. The emphasis throughout is on how networks of social relationships facilitate individual and organizational learning and goal attainment.

We begin in Chapter 1 by presenting basic terminology and examples of social network analysis applied to formal organizations.

1 Social capital and social networks in action

In this chapter we'll set forth some terminology that we'll carry forward throughout the text and foreshadow things to come by previewing the steps involved in mapping networks. We'll do the latter by providing examples of the use of social network analysis in diagnosing problems or uncovering opportunities in organizations.

1.1 Some terminology and definitions

The most fundamental concept we have to define is that of a *social tie*. A relation or tie is said to exist when there is an incidence of ongoing, repeated contact between two parties. When a tie is distinct from any formal organization, it is called a social tie, or *social relation*. There are some things worth noting about social ties:

1. They require two parties; the relations you have with yourself are not social.
2. They require *contact*, but this contact does not have to be face to face. Contact could occur via phone, email, written correspondence, text messaging, or other means.
3. The contact must be repeated, but it need not be frequent. Seeing a classmate every ten years at your reunion still constitutes a social tie.
4. The contact must be ongoing, meaning that it is subject to occurring again at some time, although such a time can be indefinite. Even if you don't know how long it will be until the next incidence of contact or exchange, but both parties are open to contact or exchange, a social tie exists.
5. In the context of a formal organization, social ties must in some way go beyond the prescribed workflow interaction. If a worker is required to report specific information to their supervisor, then the incidence of contact in which only that specific information is exchanged does not by itself constitute a social tie.
6. A *social network* is a pattern of social ties among a well-defined group of parties.

There are many kinds of social ties and thus many kinds of social networks: friendship, advice, family, collegial, just to name a handful. In general, ties can be characterized by the type of activity that is engaged in or the content of what is exchanged during incidences of contact. There is no exhaustive or exclusive typology of social ties. Any categorization should reflect the purpose of the analysis for which it is being used.

The purpose of analyzing the social networks in organizations is to understand how the *informal structure* operates in conjunction with the *formal structure* and workflow. The purpose is not to change the informal structure, nor is the purpose to change the formal structure. Either may be recommended as a result of the *network analysis*, however, as illustrated in the next section.

1.2   The company behind the chart

If our purpose is to give a good overall sense of a work organization's functioning, then, according to Krackhardt and Hanson (1993), it is useful to look at three types of networks: advice, trust, and communication. Although the terms seem straightforward, we need to be careful to understand what is meant by each of these three types, as the meanings intended are very specific and may not be what a layperson would think. So, let's look at their meanings:

- *Advice*, in solving task-related problems and obtaining technical information needed to perform one's duties. Advice, here, does not refer to one's personal troubles.
- *Trust*, in sharing confidential or political information and providing support for one's ideas or proposals at work. So, trust is separate from credibility. That is, trust refers to organizational politics and not to whether you trust the advice given about how to perform a task.
- *Communication*, about what is happening at work more generally. Seeking advice or getting trust obviously involves some form of communication. Yet we do not include these as communication ties. Instead, communication ties provide information about news or events at work, rather than how to do your job or whether someone will cover your back.

With the understanding of these definitions for advice, trust, and communication, the authors report that, in their experiences in working with actual organizations, each has proven most useful in diagnosing a particular sort of organizational problem:

- *Advice networks can uncover routine conflicts.* Routine conflicts are day-to-day, or otherwise reoccurring, disagreements over how things should be done or on what assumptions one should operate. How to do things and what information to use in doing them are elements of advice, as we've defined them. As a result, advice networks diagnose such disagreements, for example, by showing when there are fragmented sources of expertise, or no sources at all.

- *Trust networks can diagnose non-routine problems*, such as failing change efforts. Non-routine situations, by their very nature, involve uncertainty and the need to generate ideas about new things to do, or new ways of doing things, and build support for those ideas. As a result, trust as defined comes into play. By showing who is looked to for support, or who many feel will act in their interests, the trust network can help to identify good candidates for bringing the organization together to mobilize resources and marshal change.
- *Communication networks can diagnose inefficiency or low productivity.* Keeping in mind that our definition is limited to information about what is happening at work or what the organization is doing beyond one's specific tasks or company politics, consider the implications of very dense or very sparse communication networks. In the former (dense networks), workers may be spending a great deal of time and energy working the rumor mill to find out or spread the word about what is going on. This is time and energy taken away from doing their tasks and is hence inefficient. The organization could likely use formal means (memos, emails, announcements, meetings, etc.) to disseminate information more efficiently. At the other extreme (sparse networks), workers hardly talk to one another at all about what is going on. In such cases, workers may be perfectly or imperfectly informed, but either way the lack of social bonding can create morale problems, such as alienation or stress, which can impede productivity.

Just because each of the three types of networks can be most useful in diagnosing a particular sort of problem does not mean that these networks should always be used separately. These networks can, and should, often be used together to understand other problems, such as turnover, and should always be used in conjunction with the formal organization chart or workflow network both to understand the problem and to formulate and enact a solution, once a problem is diagnosed.

The optics company
This is an example of using trust and advice networks to diagnose a failing change effort and enact solutions by changing the formal structure. Our story parallels the experiences of Krackhardt and Hanson (1993) with a

Barton (CEO)

Lens Design	Mirror Lab	Materials	Control Systems
Mullaney (SVP)	Petersen (SVP)	Levy (SVP)	Conn (SVP)
Bahr	Cottrel	Blau	Hubble
Rodrigues	Lehman	Jimenez	Buchanan
Oaxaca	Angus	Andersen	Hamil
	Parsons	Olsen	
	Joseph	Mason	
	Dicke	Ztsosi	
	Taylor		
	Suarez		
	VandeVen		
	Manuel		
	Apple		

Figure 1.1   Formal organization for the optics firm

software company. We tell the story from the point of view of Barton, the CEO of an Arizona optics company. Mr. Barton is frustrated by his inability to successfully launch a new strategic direction for his company, which has four divisions: Lens Design, Mirror Lab, Materials Technologies, and Optical Control Systems. The formal organization (organization chart) is shown in Figure 1.1.

The history is that the Mirror Lab has long been the division that has generated the bulk of the company's revenues, and has seen the bulk of rewards and reinvestment as a result. Owing to changes in federal grant priorities, Barton sets out to launch a new strategy that would invest some of the revenues generated by the Mirror Lab to build up the other divisions, in hopes of expanding the company's overall position. After announcing his plan, morale in the Mirror Lab drops, with clear threats of turnover among some of the key players in that division, feeling their status, and possibly bonuses, would be lowered. Realizing he needs to bring his employees into the strategic planning process, Barton forms a task force to find a new strategic direction. As a symbolic gesture, Barton appoints a representative of the Mirror Lab, Mr. Cottrel, to chair the task force, but includes key representatives from all divisions among the members. The task force quickly breaks down, with members fiercely competing for the

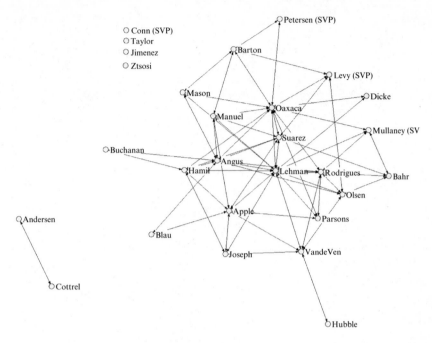

Figure 1.2   Trust network for optics firm

interests of their respective divisions, rather than working cooperatively to improve the interests of the company a whole.

As Barton wonders what has happened, he calls the local business school management department, looking for advice. Faculty with expertise on managing networks offer to help. Recognizing this as a non-routine problem (a failing change effort), they are particularly interested in the trust network as a diagnostic tool.

It is clear from the trust network map in Figure 1.2 that Cottrel, who has been asked to lead the task force, is not well trusted. This is seen because he is off on the periphery, rather than near the center of the map, and has just a single trust tie. Why, then, was he chosen to lead the change effort? To understand this, we need to look at another map: the advice network.

We see from the advice network in Figure 1.3 that Cottrel has a key role as a technical expert (which we can infer from his central position in the advice network). Barton mistook colleagues' faith in Cottrel's technical expertise (credibility) for faith that he would act in their political interests (trust). This is a good example of the importance of keeping in mind the specific, narrow definitions of advice, trust, and communication used here.

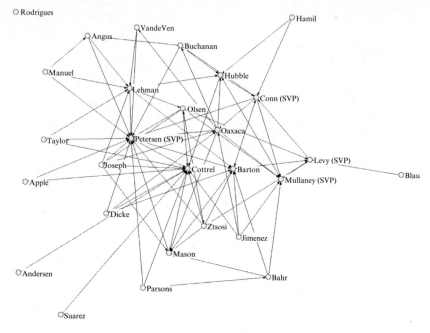

Figure 1.3   Advice network for the optics firm

To formulate and enact a solution, the consulting faculty used both of these network maps along with the organization chart. Cottrel cannot simply be dismissed, since he is such a valuable technical expert. Yet we can see from the trust network that Lehman, who is also in the Mirror Lab, is well trusted by employees throughout the company. Hence Lehman would make a good task force leader. To bring Lehman on board without insulting Cottrel is the trick. Consulting faculty devised a remedy in which Cottrel and Lehman were made co-chairs of the task force, and it was presented as a way to help relieve Cottrel of what had become a bigger job than originally anticipated. Cottrel stayed on board, and the combination of his expertise with Lehman's trust soon produced positive results. The consultants also noticed something peculiar involving Petersen, the head of the Mirror Lab. Can you diagnose the problem? Can you suggest a solution?

The realty office
Krackhardt and Hanson (1993) also describe an example of using communication networks to diagnose low productivity and inefficiency, leading to changes in the informal structure (via changes in routines and practices)

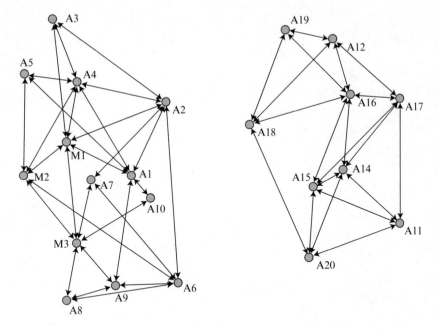

Figure 1.4   Communication network for the realty office

of a large bank. We relate a similar story that begins when a realty office conducted what was expected to be a routine customer satisfaction survey. The results showed a high level of customer complaints about a lack of timely response to questions about the office's realtors and services. The realty office's inefficient response to customer inquiries was diagnosed using the communication network.

What consulting analysts found was the network shown in Figure 1.4, a structure split into two separate subnetworks. When we have a case like this, where the subnetworks are completely disjoint, we call the subnetworks components. Looking at the network map, we find managers (denoted by M) and some agents (denoted by A) in one component and another set of agents in a second component.

What was not apparent from the initial social network map was just what was keeping the two subnetworks apart. To understand this, analysts needed to look at the formal organization alongside the communication network. Doing so revealed that the subnetworks were defined by work status. One subnetwork consisted of the full-time realtors, while the second subnetwork consisted of realtors who work only part time or intermittently. To see this visually, we color the points for each person according to their work status, light circles for full time and dark squares

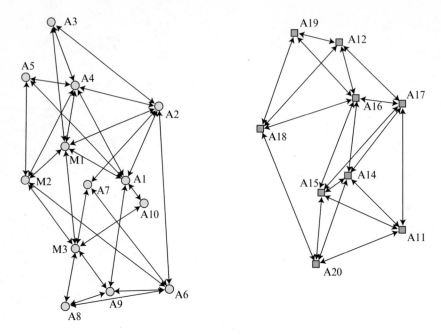

Figure 1.5   Communication network for the realty office, nodes colored by shift

for part time. The resulting network map is shown in Figure 1.5. Now it is clear that the components are defined by work status.

To understand why the communication network is imploded by work status, and how this led to customer dissatisfaction, the analysts further had to look at the organization's practices. Managing agents worked full time and all meetings were held on midweek mornings, when part-time workers were often not available. As a result, the part-time agents were not kept up to date on changes in staff, products, and services, and had difficulty in getting answers for customers, and the full-time agents were not informed about the availability and expertise of the part-time agents.

To remedy the problem, the consulting group recommended changing communication patterns to bridge the two subgroups through changes in practices. To begin, meetings were now held at the end of the day, between shifts, so that all workers could attend. In addition, workers were rotated, when possible, between the two shifts. When a worker needed a day off, they were required to contact workers from the other shift to find a substitute. These and other new practices altered the communication patterns, creating ties and leading to a more robust, single network. Customer satisfaction improved.

1.3 Potentially problematic structures

Krackhardt and Hanson (1993) identify some common structures to look for that can indicate a problem. Note, however, that they will not always be problematic if they occur in an organization.

There are five classes of potentially problematic structural features:

1. *Imploded* relationships occur when members of a formal group (department, level, etc.) have social relations only with others in the group and have no social relations with any others outside of the group.
2. *Irregular* patterns are the opposite of imploded relationships, and might well be called exploded relationships. They occur when members of a formal group have social relations only with others outside of the group and have no social relations with others in the group.
3. *Holes* occur (aside from the above examples of imploded and exploded relations) whenever two parties that would be expected, on the basis of workflow interdependence, to have a social relation of any given type fail to do so. For example, if a trainee fails to go to more experienced co-workers for advice a hole would exist. In another example, if we'd expect members of our Finance department to go to members of Accounting for cost data and they do not do so, then we might infer a hole.
4. *Bow ties*, as a form of social structure, occur when all, or most, of the social relations among a set of persons go through a single, central person. If the center of the 'bow' were lost, then any flow of communication, advice, or trust based on the informal network would cease.
5. *Fragile* structures are those that do not quite meet the strict definitions of any of the above potentially problematic structures, but nearly do so. That is, if members of a formal group have ties only with members of their own group and just one other group (in an organization with many formal groups), then the structure would be fragile. If the, perhaps few, ties to that one other group were lost, it would become imploded.

Identifying these structures is akin to finding a clue, rather than solving a puzzle. Once they are identified, the real work begins of understanding whether they reflect the proper functioning of the organization or whether they are dysfunctional. Network analysis can be harmful if used without understanding formal structure, work roles, and human capital (individuals' talent, experience, etc.). Understanding informal structures supplements, not supplants, understanding the formal structure. When the two are in conflict, whether to change the formal structure or informal relationships depends on understanding the full organizational context, including the formative bases of the social ties.

1.4   Stratified interaction networks

We now turn to a *large-scale* example. Koput and Gutek (in press) studied five cohorts of undergraduate students in an elite program during their junior and senior years. They followed the steps above to construct inter-action networks among the students. We'll read more about their study in a later chapter, but for now let's use the networks to see if we can assess problematic, or promising, structures. Figure 1.6 shows the network map for the first cohort in their study.

Before we begin reading this network map, let's think about what we need to know in order to be able to identify problematic or promising features of the structure. Clearly, we need the visualization of the structure, with individuals as nodes and ties as lines, as shown in Figure 1.6. We can tell a number of things just by looking at the structure. Yet a key lesson from the above examples is that we need more than just the network map in order to draw any conclusions. What do we also need?

Figure 1.6   Undergraduate cohort network

We need to know something about three things:

1. the formal structure of the organization;
2. the individuals;
3. the type of social relation defined in the ties.

We'll get back to those things before we think we know what is going on with this network, but now let's just look at the structure.

What do we need to know about the structure itself? To identify implosions, irregularities, and so on, we need some sense of *groupings in terms of the nodes*. But, to distinguish them from the formal groups, we'll call them regions or, if disjoint, components. Then, we need some sense of bottlenecks and vacuums – places where there seem to be an unusual *prevalence or absence of activity in terms of the lines* – to identify bow ties or holes.

In terms of node groupings, we can take notice of three different regions. There is a main region to the right, then a secondary region to the left, and finally a very small island near the top center. The island is cut off from the rest of the network, and consists of just three persons. The main and secondary regions are not disjoint, but tied together by just three threads running through just two persons in the main region and three in the secondary.

As far as line activity goes, there are a couple of places where there are a lot of lines running through a single node, such as the one that connects two actors in the secondary region to the main region. This is a possible bottleneck. On the other hand, the secondary region has two or three strands where an actor is tied in to the network only with a single thread, marking potential holes.

These features should clue us in to investigate implosions, bow ties, holes, and of course fragilities. We don't want to discount the possibility of irregularities, but we'll need to have more information pointing us in that direction. For now, the regions may represent a fragility towards imploding, dependent on a few bow ties spanning a sea of holes.

To go further, we need to bring in information about the ties, the formal organization and the individuals. The ties are general communication ties, representing who each actor talks to most frequently. As a network of undergraduate students, we might think about possible formal groupings – major, class, and so on. Here, we have a cohort from a single major, so we won't learn much else that way. We can then look at characteristics of the actors, such as age, GPA, or gender. Since gender is a nice natural grouping variable, let's try it first. Let's redraw the network map coloring the nodes by gender, in the same way we colored them by shift in the realty

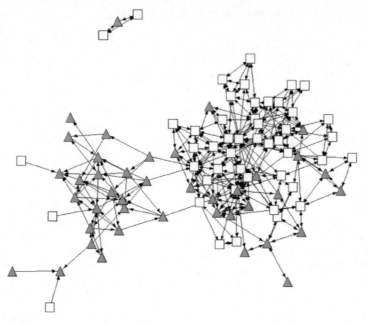

Figure 1.7   Undergraduate cohort network, colored by gender

office example. Dark triangles are women; light squares are men (Figure 1.7).

The main and secondary regions are defined to a good extent by gender: men, constituting two-thirds of the population, define the main region, and women, under-represented overall, the secondary region. Men are mostly tied to other men, while many women maintain ties only to other women. This is not a case of complete implosion, as we noted, not only because of the two bridges we spotted, but because there are a number of triangles in the squares region (and three squares in the triangles region). For the most part, the off-color nodes (e.g. triangles in the squares region) are found around the outside of the contrasting region. Women are trying to tap into the men's network, but haven't quite moved beyond the periphery. Yet many have multiple ties to men, providing some stability. The men who are part of the secondary network, while also at the periphery, are all tied in with just a single contact, which they are therefore dependent on. In this case, the absence of ties to other men should make us think of structural holes. We'll spend more time trying to understand this network later; for now we just wanted to practice identifying structures. Having done so, let's end this introductory chapter with a look forward.

1.5   Preview of steps in network analysis

Taken together, these examples show how useful mapping social networks can be for diagnosing organizational problems as well as for formulating and enacting solutions. How to perform the mapping will be covered in detail in the first part of the book, but let's give a quick preview by looking at the steps followed in these examples:

1. Map the network by conducting a network survey and preparing and processing the data. In this step, we ask members of the organization to tell us about their social relations, enter the responses and cross-check for consistency, and numerically manipulate the data to produce a visual representation of the network, such as those we viewed earlier. This step is covered in Part II.
2. Analyze the data, obtaining measures of both the overall social structure and each individual's position within the network. We'll learn how to compute these measures in Part III. We'll emphasize understanding how the computations are done and what each measure really captures, and provide references on how to implement them in the most commonly used computer software packages.
3. Interpret the results. Having mapped the network and obtained measures, we still have to interpret it in the context of the organization, in order for our analyses to have any meaning. We'll learn the concepts that will enable us to do so in a rigorous way in the rest of Part I.

2 Central concepts: social capital, strong and weak

In this chapter we'll cover some basic ideas about social capital: its properties, its forms, and the two major types, strong tie social capital and weak tie social capital.

2.1 Properties and forms of social capital

James Coleman popularized the concept of social capital in economic behavior in his paper 'Social capital in the creation of human capital' (1988). We are going to be more concerned with what Coleman tells us about social capital itself than about its role in the creation of human capital. Coleman reviews some properties of social capital and then provides examples to illustrate the productive value in social relations. The examples also allow us to understand the forms of social capital and how network structure influences these forms.

Properties

We'll begin with four key properties of social capital. We start by parsing the term into its components, taken in reverse order: capital and social. Capital is a productive resource that can be invested to produce value. This is true of financial capital as well as human capital (your talents, experience, education, and so on). We expect the same of social capital. The social part implies that it belongs not to individuals, but to a social structure, be it an organization, community, or other social grouping. As such, social capital stems from relationships between social actors, rather than the endowments of the actors themselves.

Social capital is:

- a *productive resource* that can be used to create value;
- an *investment*, with an element of risk the value is not assured and will accrue in the future rather than being immediate;
- *inherent in relationships*, not actors, meaning that it does not belong to one person, but requires a social structure and joint participation;
- *appropriable*, meaning that a relationship of one type (say work) may be used for other purposes (say friendship) – although it is not

16

completely fungible, meaning that it cannot be cashed in on demand for a predetermined value that's not specific to certain activities, time, or context.

Coleman presents four examples of productive value in social relations. These demonstrate the properties just presented and also highlight the forms of social capital that we'll review below.

We begin with a story about wholesale diamond brokers in New York. What's interesting is that, when one of these brokers is looking to sell diamonds, they will give possibly hundreds of thousands of dollars in diamonds to a prospective buyer without any inventory, receipt or bonding (insurance). There's value in this strange behavior because it allows these brokers to make deals more quickly and at lower cost than brokers in other markets against whom they, as a community, are competing. This gives them a competitive advantage in selling to retailers. But why do they trust each other so much? Coleman ties this trust to the fact that they are a community rather than just a market. That is, the market is superimposed on an existing social structure. The brokers are not only business associates; they are members of the same synagogue, they are interrelated, and they live in the same neighborhood.

A story about South Korean study circles indicates that the study circles share these features. In South Korea during the 1980s political dissent was not permitted. Yet rallies in opposition to government policies were well organized and attended. How did this organization occur in the face of government oppression? It was not a simple matter to pass along information about such events, since you might inadvertently pass it on to a government agent acting undercover trying to infiltrate the opposition. Such risks were lessened by using existing social structures to mobilize political dissent. Subversive groups met in the guise of student study circles, in which only those who came from the same family, church, or hometown school were invited to join. This insight remains relevant in the 2000s, as similar study circles operate in Iran and elsewhere.

Coleman tells a third story that seems to provoke the question: Why would a single mother move from suburban Detroit to Jerusalem for the safety of her child. In Jerusalem, because of the historical and current circumstances, there is a strong norm among adults to look after children – anyone's children. Hence, she could let her child go to the park confident that any adults in the area would view it as their responsibility to supervise her child. This is productive because it allows the mom to work or perform chores rather than sit at the park. There is value here as well, since it saves the cost of a babysitter, nanny, or daycare service.

In the street markets in Nogales, Sonora, vendors perform somewhat remarkable favors for one another. A typical story goes something like the following, and parallels Coleman's observations of the Khan El Khalili market of Cairo. Suppose you are in a glass store because a member of your party is looking at some merchandise. Another member of your party asks you in a normal voice if you know of any wood carving shops in the area. The proprietor interrupts, apologizing for overhearing. She knows of a good wood carver and offers to bring you some merchandise from that seller to look at. When you show some interest, since you are waiting anyway, she leaves you and your party unattended in her shop and disappears out a back door, returning in a few minutes with a box of carvings that belong to another vendor. She has done so without need to leave a receipt or collateral. Indeed, when your friend finds a piece he likes, she haggles with him, settles on a price, then takes his money and gives him the piece – all as though it was her own merchandise. While not her merchandise, it was that of a merchant with family and hometown ties. The value here is similar to that in the diamond broker story – there is a saving of time and money that keeps the customer in their market, whereas you might well have gone across the way to a block of competing merchants.

These stories clearly illustrate the properties of social capital – that it is a productive resource, as described. It's an investment, in friendships and in community, familial, church or school activities which are later appropriated. And it is inherent in relationships and the social structure that arises from them. The stories also allow us to highlight three forms, or substances, of social capital.

Forms, or substances

- *Obligations.* These are the credit slips you give when someone else does a good turn for you and which you receive when you do a good turn for another. Take the street market story, for example. When one merchant goes out of her way to sell the carvings of another, this creates a credit slip that she can redeem. Obviously, the carver might facilitate a sale of glass for the merchant, but these credits are often more valuable if they can be cashed in by anyone else in the social structure helping her out, rather than only by the woodcarver. The extent to which this form of social capital develops depends in the first instance on the level of trust between the two merchants, the glass seller and the woodcarver, and in the second instance on the overall sense of trustworthiness in the environment.
- *Information channels.* These are the grapevines that provide needed or usable information or advice. Take the study group story, for example. These groups allowed students to learn about when and where the next rally or protest would occur and what actions were

required to organize the opposition. This is information that is not otherwise available except at great risk. The extent to which channels of information are a form of social capital depends on the cost of information acquisition and surveillance, as well as on how up to date the partners are. That is, if the information is readily available in the media or through other formal channels, then there is little capital in exchanging it socially. Likewise, if your contacts do not have the latest information, if the information is subject to change, then these exchanges are not valuable.

- *Norms.* These are the codes of conduct – that is, expectations for, or standards of, behavior – that arise from group interaction. Take the Jerusalem story, for example, where a strong norm exists in that all adults are expected to watch over any and all children in their vicinity. Clearly, these are a form of social capital, since watching others' children frees the parents to engage in productive tasks. Norms differ from credit slips in that you may do so not for tit-for-tat return of favor (you may not even have children, but be expected to watch over them). Instead, norms are reinforced through support, status, or other rewards, as well as through sanctions (punishments for someone who fails to follow the norm).

Getting back to social structure, all of these forms of social capital have, to some extent, different contingencies: trust for obligations, costs for information, rewards for norms, and so on. But these things depend, in turn, on network structure. We'll detail two characteristics of structure that influence social capital: closure and multiplexity.

Characteristics of structure

Closure means that a social structure resides within a closed loop. In other words, say you have two friends. If they know each other, then there is closure in your small network. If they do not, but they each have friends who know one another, then again there is closure, and so forth. Looking at a network map, you would be able to trace one or more loops. If there is no point at which your friends' friends know each other, then there is no closure. Looking at a network map, you would not be able to trace a loop. Of course, there are degrees of closure. If there are many loops, then there is more closure than if there are few loops.

Closure in a network allows members to:

- repute obligations: you can develop a reputation that your credit slips are good, so that more others will accept them not only directly from you but from those to whom you are obliged;

- verify information: you can check for consistency at different ends of a loop;
- sanction violations of norms: you can prevent a person from accessing other partners, rather than only withholding your own tie to them.

Multiplexity means that any given pair of partners will often have more than one type of tie. For instance, the diamond brokers had business, family, church, and community ties. Hence, both dyadic relations and the overall social structure can be described as multiplex.

Multiplexity in a network performs several functions:

- It facilitates closure, since a loop can be formed by stringing together ties of different types for different pairs.
- It allows appropriability, since there are more types of ties available.
- It magnifies the impact of sanctions, since there is more to take away from a violator.

Losing business ties is bad, but losing your family, friends, and church, and having to move out of your neighborhood all at the same time really hurts. When social ties are embedded in a social structure that has closure and multiplexity, we refer to them as strong ties. We also use the term 'cohesive' for such ties. So, from Coleman, we can say that there are advantages, or strengths, in strong, or cohesive, ties. Strong, cohesive ties help mobilize and build resources, whether we are talking about social, human, or economic capital.

2.2   Social relativism

The strong tie social capital described by Coleman belongs to a collective, and serves to further the goals of the collective in competition with other collectives. Such social capital is a property of the relationships in the social structure that connect members of the collective, and is not the property of any individual member. Members can, all the same, draw on it to help build, or protect, their own human or economic capital. A study by Baker and Faulkner (1993) provides a dramatic example of the point that social capital is a productive good from the standpoint of the collective from whose social relations it stems and not in any absolute, universal, or objective sense.

Baker and Faulkner studied what they termed illegal networks in the heavy electrical equipment industry. These networks were illegal in the sense that the productive use to which they were put by the collective defining the social structure (the heavy electrical equipment industry) was against the laws of another collective: the United States government.

The productive, but illegal, use was price fixing, and different network structures were successful, in different ways, at 1) concealing the conspiracies from outsiders, and 2) protecting the top executives from prosecution once the conspiracies were unraveled. Indeed, Baker and Faulkner found that the network structures were 'driven primarily by the need to maximize concealment, rather than the need to maximize [information processing] efficiency' (p. 837), in that they were largely decentralized and nonhierarchical. In Coleman's terms, decentralized, nonhierarchical networks would be higher in closure and multiplexity.

The decentralized networks concealed more extensive illegal activities for a longer time period than the network in the more centralized conspiracy. Further, top executives in the decentralized conspiracies avoided successful prosecution.

There was one case that involved a more centralized network. According to Baker and Faulkner, interestingly, participants in the centralized conspiracy 'were much less likely to be found guilty' than were actors in the more decentralized networks (p. 845). This odd finding becomes more sensible when actor rank and centrality are jointly taken into account; in the centralized network, top executives are more likely to be found guilty, whereas in the decentralized network middle managers – who are more central in the informal organization – take the fall.

2.3   The strength of weak ties
We earlier defined the strength of ties as a function of the overall properties of the social structure. This may seem a bit odd, since we normally think of the *strength* of a tie between two people as a combination of:

- frequency and duration of interactions;
- intensity of emotional attachment;
- level of intimacy, or closeness (although we'll reserve the term 'closeness' for our measure of centrality);
- volume (e.g. of communication, advice, or support) exchanged;

among other factors.

Yet these factors are difficult to measure, particularly when we are trying to map a network to diagnose organizational problems or identify opportunities. So let's tie together our common-sense understanding of what makes a tie strong and the properties of the larger social structure. That is, how do time, emotional involvement, and so on produce a structure with closure and multiplexity?

To answer this question, Granovetter (1973) offers the following hypothesis. The stronger the tie between two actors, A and B, the larger the proportion of other actors to which they will both be tied. This is so for three reasons:

1. *Time capacity.* First, we all have only so much time we can devote to social interaction. The stronger the tie you have to one individual, say B, then the more time you spend with him or her. Now let's introduce person C, to whom you also have a tie. The stronger this tie becomes, the more time you spend with person C. At some point, you will reach your time capacity and, for either tie to become even stronger, you will have to share time with both B and C, thus introducing a tie between them. For example, you might invite both to lunch so that you can spend time with each, but by your doing so they are now spending time with each other as well as with you.

2. *Homophily and influence.* A long tradition of social research has demonstrated that we form ties with others with whom we share attributes or affiliations. That is, we interact socially with others with whom we have common interests, which may be based on our demographics, location, or participation. For example, let's say you really like to watch basketball. Now, you may have many co-workers, but you are more likely to interact socially with those who also like to watch basketball. This is called homophily, the tendency for 'birds of a feather to flock together'. When those who spend time together develop common interests, we call this social influence. Regardless of which way the causation goes, we can explain Granovetter's argument by running with the basketball example. If you are A and there are two others who like to watch basketball, B and C, then not only are you more likely to form ties with them but they are more likely to form a tie with each other, irrespective of their ties to you.

3. *Cognitive balance.* Finally, Granovetter draws on social psychology to argue that theories of balance support his hypothesis. Let's say that you have such a strong tie to B that you are B's best friend. Also say you have such a strong tie to C that you are C's best friend. Now, who is your best friend? Suppose B and C are unacquainted, but aware of each other. In some sense, a competition to be your best friend occurs, and B and C may each attempt to undermine the relationship you have with the other, owing to envy or other psychological factors. This puts you in an unbalanced position, because you have positive affect for both B and C, but they have animosity for each other. As a result, you will either need to weaken one of the ties or bring B and C together.

For these reasons, if A has a strong tie to B, and A has a strong tie to C, then the absence of a tie between B and C is unlikely. Granovetter calls the situation where a triad consists of two strongly tied dyads and a dyad with no tie as the Forbidden Triad. In reality, such triads are not forbidden but increasingly unlikely as tie strength increases.

If Granovetter's hypothesis is correct, then *no strong tie is a bridge* (that is, no strong tie can connect otherwise unconnected actors). Stated differently, *all bridges are weak ties.*

There are two implications of this conclusion that we will be concerned with. First, looking at *triads* can help assess the strength of dyadic ties. If a triad has only two connected dyads, we can infer that at least one of them is weak, perhaps both. Conversely, if all three dyads within a triad are connected, then we'd infer that at least one, if not all, of the ties is strong. It may be difficult to get respondents to divulge the strength of their ties, and their assessments of tie strength are subject to greater bias than their assessment of whether a tie exists.

Second, we can infer that the strength, in the sense of advantage, of weak ties is in providing novel information. Here's why. Because you have strong ties with others who you spend time with and have common interests with, you also likely tap into the same primary sources of information: you watch the same news channel or read the same papers or visit the same websites. If so, then your interaction with them reinforces the information you already have, rather than providing novel information. It is through weak ties – the ties you have to those you spend less time with and have less in common with – that you gain exposure to information and viewpoints that you would not have received were it not for these social connections. Granovetter cites evidence to support this idea from innovation and job acquisition studies. The former find that innovations are often initiated by those at the periphery of organizations, whereas the latter suggest that new jobs are more often found through acquaintances than close friends.

2.4   The productive value: primary, secondary, and tertiary
Ron Burt is a leading scholar in the field of social networks, who is concerned with the value, or benefits, of social capital for individuals who are in strategic competition. Burt agrees with Coleman that social capital is distinct from human capital or economic, that is, financial, capital as a property of social structure rather than individual attributes. Burt (1992, 1997) goes further in theorizing that social capital acts multiplicatively with respect to human and economic capital to alter the rate of return an individual receives from their investments in human and economic capital. That is, you cannot substitute social capital for human or economic capital,

and vice versa. You need social capital along with human or economic capital in order to get an above average return from your investment.

We need to note here that Burt and Coleman are concerned with two different things. Coleman is interested in how social capital can be used for the betterment of a collective, through mobilizing resources that build human and economic capital. Burt, alternatively, is concerned with how individuals can use their social capital to outcompete others within an organization or group, by allowing them to make the best use of their human or economic capital.

The difference between Coleman and Burt may become a bit clearer if we go through the two categories of benefits of social capital in strategic, competitive settings that concern Burt: 1) information-related and 2) control-related.

Information and control
Information-related benefits of social capital include three interrelated categories:

1.   There is greater *access* to information, since you can tap into the channels formed by social connections, for both retrieving and disseminating information. Via social ties you can send or receive information that will not or cannot be transmitted through formal mechanisms.
2.   Improved *timing* of information results from a better position in the social network. You can use your social position to learn of and respond to opportunities before others.
3.   Third-party *referrals* occur when others spread information about you on your behalf – nominating you for a raise or promotion with a good reference is an example. Note that you need not even be aware if or when such a referral occurs.

All three categories of information-related benefits require *contacts* (information channel) and *reliable flow* (due to obligations, norms). They each involve more than one of the forms of social capital spelled out by Coleman.

Control-related benefits of social capital can be understood by reference to the Latin notion of the *tertius gaudens*, which translates as the 'third who benefits'. So how does a third party benefit? There are two ways, according to Burt: 1) by being between two players after the same information or resources; 2) by being between two players in multiple roles with conflicting demands.

The first is straightforward enough. If you are between two players in an information network, then you have control over which of those parties, if either, receives information. You can open or close the flow of information at will. So, if you have information, or an information channel, that two others want and cannot get without going through you, then you can play them off against each other and extract a price for brokering the information.

The second is a bit more complex, but we can understand it in terms of what would happen if a student had two final exams scheduled for the same time. The instructors are then the others that the student is between (assuming they are not communicating about the student). By showing each instructor that there is another exam at the same time, the student can essentially choose which exam to take as scheduled and which to postpone. The benefit in choosing is to take the exam that the student is best prepared for and postpone the one which may need more study time. If you find yourself in an analogous position on the job, you can perform the task that you are better at, hence improving your overall performance and thus your chances at a bonus or promotion.

Both of these tertius gaudens strategies require *uncertainty over formal authority* in order to produce any benefit. In the first, if you are required by the nature of your job to deliver the information from or to one of the parties, then you have no leverage to extract any additional benefit beyond not being fired. In the second, if one demand comes from your boss and the other from a colleague, then it is pretty clear that you perform the task asked by your boss, even if it is something you are not as good at. In our final exam example, if there is a university policy that you take the exam for the course that, say, has a larger enrollment, then you will take it as scheduled whether you are best prepared for it or not.

The problem of redundancy
To further his arguments, Burt observes that natural network expansion occurs through strong ties begetting strong ties. To understand this, let's go back to the process of *homophily*, which is key. Homophily implies that we form ties with others who are like us in some way: whether in terms of demographic factors, attitudes, affiliations, or interests. The greater the similarity between two persons who make up a dyad, the stronger the tie is likely to be. Each is likely also to have ties to others which are homophilous. Hence, as Granovetter told us, there is a basis for a tie to form between us and our friends' friends. Given the similarity between us and our friends' friends, ties that form are often strong ones. This is what is meant by strong ties begetting strong ties: a new strong tie forms between two persons on the basis of their prior strong relationships with a common partner.

The development of strong tie networks such as Burt predicts can be traced back to what Coleman told us: strong ties reproduce into a social structure with closure and multiplexity. For a community, such structural features are advantageous in mobilizing the resources of the overall group. But, if the individuals are competing with others in the network, then these features may be disadvantageous for any particular individual.

From an information-related perspective, which Burt adopts, strong ties beget redundancy of two sorts:

1. by *cohesion*, which is primary redundancy, in which we have ties to others who are themselves tied, so that any information we could get from one of them we could also get from any other.
2. by *equivalence*, which is secondary redundancy, in which we have ties to others who are in turn tied to the same set of other persons, so that each of them acts as an intermediary to the same others after some number of steps.

In either primary (cohesion) or secondary (equivalence) redundancy, we are maintaining a number of strong ties to get the information which would come with any one of them. In other words, a single tie to a member of a redundant set will give us access to information of the set. Additional ties take up our time and energy, but provide us with no new information-related benefit. That is, they do not increase the effective size of our ego network. Of course, it's nice to have more contacts, so what is the real problem?

Problem: the cost of maintaining strong ties closes you out of *nonredundant* contacts. They are a source of network constraint. With the time and energy you spend in maintaining those additional, redundant ties to the same group, you could be developing ties to persons in other groups which are not connected, by either cohesion or equivalence, to the same information pool. Nonredundant ties would provide you with novel information. Your ties to any group might not be as strong, but keep in mind here that Burt assumes you are competing against others, for compensation and promotion, rather than trying to make friends (so to speak).

Having ties to nonredundant sets of persons makes you a bridge. So not only do you have information that you would not otherwise have if you maintained redundant ties, but you are in a position to have a unique combination of information that could prove advantageous, giving you some innovative capability that is difficult to imitate since it arises from your social ties rather than your formal training or position. In network parlance, you bridge a *structural hole* identified by either a lack of cohesiveness or a lack of equivalence among your contacts.

A contingency in Burt's reasoning should be pointed out at this point, before you conclude that you should cultivate only weak ties to disparate others. You not only need the information channel provided by the contact, whether weak or strong. You also need your contacts to be motivated to provide you with the access, timing, and referrals. If you have always been merely an acquaintance, such motivation may well not exist.

Strategic networking, it follows, requires tact in two ways:

1. To develop reliable flow requires stronger ties, so that others are motivated to act on your behalf or in your interest.
2. To reach more nonredundant contacts requires weaker ties, since strong ties take up more of your time capacity per tie.

Let's consider some additional contingencies.

Contingencies
In combining the ideas of Coleman, Granovetter, and Burt, we can conclude that the advantages of strong versus weak ties depend on the *content* of the ties, the *stage of development* of your social capital, and the overall *objectives* for using social capital. Let's look at these:

- *Content* matters. Strong ties would be wanted for trust or support ties, but weak ties would serve well for advice, once reliable flow is established.
- *Stage* matters. Even where weak ties would serve well, reliable flow must be established, and this requires initially investing in a stronger relationship and then allowing it to weaken naturally (through diminished investments) over time.
- *Objective* matters. Where community level outcomes are pursued, stronger ties produce an advantageous social structure. Where individuals pursue outcomes in competition, weak ties provide information-related benefits.

Burt has conducted a number of scientific studies to demonstrate the validity of his ideas. In one study, he hypothesized that the weak tie social capital, which provides information and control benefits, is a function of ego network properties (that is, the properties of the network formed by your contacts and the ties among them). He initially looked at these three properties:

1. size – the number of contacts;
2. density – the percentage of dyads to which you are tied that are themselves tied;

3. hierarchy – the amount of differentiation in formal authority, or the extent to which information must flow through a central person (e.g. the boss).

The findings of this study show the following:

- Small, dense, hierarchical ego networks constrain, or limit, the information-related benefits accruing to the focal ego.
- Large, sparse, decentralized ego networks create opportunity by providing more information-related benefits. In this study, benefits are measured in terms of their returns in the form of earlier promotions and larger bonuses.

These returns to social capital are further contingent on characteristics of the formal organization, not just the social network. In this study, weak tie social capital was more valuable for those at lower ranks and depended on the department a person was in along with the number of peers (those doing the same work). Those with more peers doing the same work found their social capital to be less valuable. The more others in the same job category as you, the less you can utilize your social ties to garner bonuses and promotions.

This finding is quite interesting, since we could also say that the fewer others who do the same work, the more you need to develop social ties to get compensation and promotion. If there are many workers in a job category, it is likely that the company has formal policies that guide compensation and promotion, thus negating the influence of social influence, whereas if your work is unique then it may not pay for the company to formalize your career ladder, and your value to the company (and you) may go unnoticed unless you make some noise through the megaphone provided by the social network.

2.5   The tertius iungens orientation

Obstfeld (2005) takes a different view from that of Burt when it comes to the role of being a broker in a social network. While Burt focused on the control-related benefits of keeping others apart, Obstfeld points out the potential benefit of introducing others who are otherwise not directly connected. To understand this argument, let's take the case of two others, although it could well apply to groups of others.

If two parties have information or resources that are valuable, but incomplete, then introducing the parties can allow them to combine their information or resources in productive ways, leading to the creation of value. If you introduced them, your role may establish an obligation on their part either to return the favor in kind at some later date or, of particular interest here, to include you in the returns, paying you a finder's fee, in a sense. Obstfeld refers to the person introducing others as the *tertius iungens*, which translates from Latin as the 'third who joins'. While joining others with complementary information or resources can provide value in many ways, Obstfeld is particularly interested in the case where innovation results.

Innovation is a special case because it by definition requires a *novel* combination of information or resources. Thus parties with a given piece of information or given resource may not be able to identify what other information or resource will combine with theirs to produce a valued outcome. This is different from situations in which, if I have a skill and a task to perform, I can usually identify the other skills needed to succeed.

For instance, as a professor, if I am skilled in analyzing data, I may recognize that I need a partner with a skill in thinking about theory in order to create a good research paper. In this case, I may be able to find a partner to join up with readily enough, without a third party being involved.

But, in the case of innovation, I may have some information that I don't even recognize as valuable, because not only don't I have the other information or resources needed to turn it into an innovative idea or product but I couldn't specify what such resources are beforehand. It is in the case of innovation, then, that a third party who is aware of the set of information and resources possessed by a group of actors in a social structure has a special advantage in identifying parties whose introduction could create a spark. Because of the savvy displayed by the finder in seeing the potential for value in novel combinations that others had not recognized, those who are joined are likely to seek the continued involvement of the third party. The result is that the tertius iungens shares in the ultimate returns, if the innovation is successful.

Obstfeld (2005) views the tertius iungens as a 'strategic behavioral orientation by which actors bring forth such [novel] combinations and recombinations' (p. 102) of other actors and, hence, resources and information. Explicating, he identifies two iungens strategies in which the finder or broker may engage: brief and sustained.

In the *brief iungens* strategy, the broker may 'introduce or facilitate ties between parties in such a way that the coordinative role of the tertius iungens subsequently recedes in importance' (p. 104). In other words, you introduce them, making sure they understand each other and the potential value in their combination, and then let them be.

Sustained iungens involves introducing or facilitating ties and then continuing to coordinate the actions of the parties over time. When it comes to innovative joining, sustained iungens seems most likely to prevail. A result of this sustained iungens activity is that the broker will be creating a social structure that is more dense and has fewer structural holes, while increasing involvement in innovation.

Obstfeld finds support for his ideas in a study in an engineering division of a large automotive manufacturer. A tertius iungens orientation and dense social networks, along with diverse social knowledge, predicted involvement in innovation. On the surface, this result seems to contradict Burt, who maintains that bridging structural holes is the key to innovative potential. A resolution is, thankfully, at hand if we consider the time dimension. The network of the tertius iungens is replete with structural holes that have been filled by their own hand. Hence, bridging structural holes is a necessary precondition to enacting a tertius iungens orientation.

2.6 Bandwidth and echo

Burt attempts to reconcile his argument that only weak ties provide social capital with the apparent value in cohesion by acknowledging that closure, through strong ties, is sometimes important to realizing the value of weak ties and, in particular, structural holes. Closure helps, as we learned earlier, in building trust and establishing reliable flow through the information channel provided, for Burt, by a bridging tie.

He advances his argument by showing 'how the trust associated with closure is more complex, and less salutary, than argued in [strong tie] models of social capital' (Burt, 2001, p. 2). Burt (2001) offers two hypotheses that describe how information gets exchanged in strong ties: 1) bandwidth and 2) echo. Let's take a look at these in turn, keeping in mind that the emphasis for Burt is, as before, on information as the singular substance of social capital.

The bandwidth hypothesis is, essentially, that information flow is enhanced with tie strength. The result is analogous to having a broadband connection for, say, your internet, rather than dial-up. More information, greater in volume and richer in nature, gets transmitted, and communication is more two-way. In the early internet days, by analogy, downloads were slow and text based, while uploads were not even possible. Today, uploads and downloads of all media, text, audio, and video, are not only possible but increasingly fast.

The increased bandwidth comes from investment in an infrastructure of closure and multiplexity. To recapitulate our earlier lesson, these structural features that we labeled cohesion provide information verification, reputation building, and enforcement of sanctions, the key building blocks of social trust.

The dynamics are worth noting. We are in a social circle with other actors; some we know and some we do not know. We hear, through word of mouth, about those we do not know, as those we know will also know some others we do not. If we have strong ties, two results follow:

1. We will be embedded in a structure of closure and multiplexity with those we do not know.
2. We will likely share characteristics with those we do know, because of the tendency for homophily and social influence. We will, it follows, hear more about those we do not know from those we know well enough to think they share our own beliefs, values, and so forth.

These two results combine to suggest we will be increasingly 1) accurate and 2) confident in our information about others.

Yet the information we get from our close allies is likely to be redundant, and we are not likely to recognize just how much and in what ways. In particular, those we know well may echo, in Burt's terms, our own information and views. Failure to incorporate that into our opinions and decisions amplifies our judgments. If we are favorably predisposed to someone we do not know, we will become trusting, even if we shouldn't. Likewise, if we are disposed to doubt, then we will breed our suspicion even if trust is warranted.

Burt states: 'echo results from etiquette biasing the information that third parties disclose to ego' (2001, p. 11). Let's take a moment to understand this. In casual conversation within the workplace, you generally do not want to seem disagreeable or contrarian. Rather, you'd be disposed to agree with others, *except when both you and they recognize an asymmetry* in the information you possess. That is, if both you and an alter are aware that you have different primary sources of information, then you would be more disposed to disagree or find fault with a belief or opinion they espoused, since you have an impersonal basis for doing so. This is, of course, more likely the case when you have a weak tie to them.

If you have a strong tie with them, then you likely share primary sources of information and, since you can assume they have access to the critical bits but hold their beliefs anyway, you might tend to let their comments pass. To the extent that the emotional component of the relation is important to you, which occurs in strong ties, you might well feign agreement in order to preserve your bond. You may do so simply because correcting them is outside of your social role. Your role is to support their positions and decisions, not to influence the direction they take. The echo hypothesis is, in these terms, that if such a dynamic occurs it does so more for strong ties than weak ties.

For evidence, Burt (2001) reports the results of three studies. Combined, the studies involved more than 900 senior level employees, managers, bankers, and staff officers at four firms ranging from electronics manufacturing to financial services.

In this chapter, we have covered the central concepts in social capital, including its properties, substances, and main types: weak tie and strong tie. We also discussed the benefits of each type of social capital and considered alternate strategies for developing and managing social capital and increasing the returns it provides.

In the next chapter, we will take a look at the ways that organizations can manage and reap benefits from social capital, both internally and externally.

3 Sociocentric perspectives with applications to human resources

In this chapter we examine how a company can tap into the social capital in the informal networks formed by employees' social ties and use that social capital to further organizational goals. We consider first the case where a company is filling vacancies by promoting from within, known as internal staffing. Then we'll look at how a company can use employees' extraorganizational social networks to more effectively hire new employees from outside the organization.

INTRAORGANIZATIONAL SOCIAL CAPITAL

3.1 Filling vacancies from within

Marsden and Gorman (1999) are concerned with the nature and determinants of *internal staffing* procedures that draw on social capital versus more formal methods. Let's first identify social capital methods and formal methods so we can contrast the advantages and disadvantages of each type. Then we'll look at how a manager can determine which type of method to use in filling a vacancy, based on which is more likely to manifest its advantages.

Social capital methods are those that utilize employees' social connections to identify candidates to fill the vacant position. For our purpose here, we can identify social capital methods as either direct contacts or referrals. *Direct contacts* come from actual observation of a candidate at work, based on having an existing social tie. So they are persons either that you have had the opportunity to supervise or whose supervisor is in your social network, and so you have observed them in the course of your social interaction with their supervisor. *Referrals* come from third parties who have observed a candidate at work and nominate them to you on their behalf. Generally, the third party is someone in your social network. This makes them a credible source if you know them to have supervised the candidate first-hand or to have a strong social tie to the candidate.

Formal methods are those that apply universalistic criteria to the entire eligible workforce. The most common formal methods for internal staffing are 1) job posting and 2) seniority or merit systems. *Job posting* is where the job opening is announced in a manner accessible to all eligible employees, such as a bulletin board or, nowadays, website. Employees then submit application materials for consideration, to be weighed against specified criteria that are included in the posting. *Seniority or merit systems* are in some sense automated staffing devices, as they apply a criterion, such as length of service or average performance appraisal ratings. A system is in place to identify the eligible employee who has the highest score on the criterion and then automatically promote that person.

Social capital methods have some advantages when compared to formal methods of internal staffing. Social capital methods:

- *limit search*, to your direct contacts and those of others whose judgments you consider credible;
- *provide richer, trusted information*, because you have a much larger period of observation, having seen the person work on a day-to-day basis either directly or through a credible contact;
- *are more strategic* – since the people are in your social network, you may be able to count on them, for communication, advice, or support (trust), once they are in their new position.

Formal methods, by contrast, rely on thin information that can be contained in an application and often apply a universalistic criterion that does not actually relate to performance. In some cases, as we noted earlier, it is difficult to specify the criteria for selection, making formal methods awkward to apply.

On the other hand, formal methods do have advantages when conditions are appropriate. The advantages of formal methods stem from three features of such methods. Formal methods:

1. *apply universalistic criteria*, making the decision what would be called routine or programmed. As a result, staffing can be handled professionally and becomes predictable and defensible;
2. *appear equitable and rational*, because any eligible employee can apply, and all who apply are judged on the same specified criteria;
3. *provide advancement opportunities to outsiders*, because the programmed nature of the decision depersonalizes the process, relieving both the applicants and the hiring staff of the possibility of hurt feelings. The open eligibility allows those with minority status to advance based on known criteria, seniority, or merit.

Hence disadvantages of social capital methods, by contrast, are that they can in fact be subject to prejudice and favoritism and, even if they are not so abused, they may appear arbitrary and capricious to those who are not promoted.

Since both kinds of methods have advantages and disadvantages, determining which to use is a matter of identifying when the job being filled is such that the advantages of one type of method are more likely to occur than those of the other type of method. Based on their studies, Marsden and Gorman (1999) believe that there are six *job factors* that determine whether hiring authorities should use social capital methods or formal methods for internal staffing.

The six job factors are listed below, along with the indicator that hiring authorities can use to measure the job factor and the conditions under which social capital methods are favored. Any other conditions would favor formal methods of internal staffing.

The first job factor is *mutual adjustment*, which refers to a worker's ability to adapt his or her daily activities based on what others around him or her are doing. For example, consider an administrative team in which on any given day there is some combination of scheduling, word processing, copying, note taking, faxing, shipping, and database work to be done. Imagine also that there is no clear division of this labor in each person's job description, so that on any given day you, as a member of the team, might perform any of these tasks, depending on what others have taken care of that day. The indicator for whether a position will involve mutual adjustment is the job description. If the job description is fairly vague or flexible, rather than highly specialized and specific, then social capital methods would be favored for filling the vacancy.

The second and third job factors are *interpersonal and non-routine decision-making skills*. An interviewer can get only a small sample of these skills when formal methods are used, whereas social capital methods allow one to have observed a candidate working and dealing with others and handling unusual events over a period of time. The occupation of the job vacancy is a good indicator of the degree of interpersonal skills needed, whereas the level of the position is a good indicator of whether non-routine decision-making skills are needed. Professional jobs, along with positions in sales and client service, require the former skills, while managerial posts require the latter, and so social capital methods would be favored for internally staffing such vacancies.

The *costs of making a selection error* – that is, hiring the wrong person – and the *costs of the search* itself are the next two job factors. A selection error is costly if the company has to invest a significant amount of resources into the new employee, because of extensive on-the-job training, for example. If the person does not work out, then those skills – and the resources invested in the training – literally walk out the door (or perhaps to another floor, if the person is simply demoted back to their original position). The greater the company-specific on-the-job training, the more advantageous the use of social capital methods, whereas if formal education or professional certification suffice then formal methods would be favored. As to the costs of the search itself, social capital methods become difficult to employ if the company is sited at more than one location, since the networks of different sites are likely to have fewer links across than within. Formal methods, by contrast, can readily be used for multi-sited companies, since websites or memoranda posting the jobs have little marginal cost per extra site. The same can be said for seniority or strict merit systems. Databases do not even need to be electronically merged, since each site could simply produce its top candidate with their score, and the choice of the highest score from this group would produce the winner.

The final job factor is the *need for legitimacy*. There are some cases where the appearance of any potential for favoritism or prejudice simply cannot be abided. In such cases, formal methods must be used. While one would think that public sector or unionized companies would be indicators of the need to have the appearance of legitimacy, this turns out not to be so, according to Marsden and Gorman's (1999) work. Instead, the single important indicator is whether the company has professional human resource managers. Where a personnel department exists, formal methods are often required by the HRM staff, whereas social capital methods perform well when a company lacks a personnel department.

3.2   Forming teams

While homophily tends to occur naturally in social relations, *heterophily* is more often the result of purposive design. Prescriptions for the composition of work teams often stress the need for demographic diversity as a selection criterion. The core idea is that workers of dissimilar characteristics, be they age, tenure, gender, ethnicity, functional background, or whatnot, will have access to a wider range of information, resources, and perspectives than will workers of similar demography. In terms of social capital, such heterophilous workers would likely have internal ties (to other team members) that are weak, and thus have external ties that tap into a broad range of nonredundant pools of information and resources. While it is the network ties that ultimately provide the team capital, managers often use demographic diversity as a design principle as, for pragmatic reasons, demography is easier to assess than network position.

Reagans, Zuckerman, and McEvily (2004) argue, however, that forming work teams based on demographic diversity may backfire, for two reasons. First, but secondarily, they note that the informal networks within some organizations may not be as homophilous as other social networks. Organizational experiences and cultures can lessen homophily. Yet the lack of homophily as a universal social principle in work organizations does not deny that it is a persistent underlying force. Many work organizations are indeed marked by high degrees of homophily where it matters most (e.g. at the top).

Second, and primarily, Reagans and his colleagues hark back to the two types of social capital. They note that the prescription for demographic diversity rests solely on the notion of improving team performance via bridging ties outside of the team – providing weak tie social capital. Strong tie social capital is overlooked as an important team asset. Strong ties inside of the team create the cohesion needed to mobilize members' attention and coordinate their efforts towards a common good. Yet a demographically diverse team is, other considerations aside, likely to have weak internal ties. As a result, teams must be made based on the network contacts, rather than the demography, of members. Internal network density should be jointly maximized with external network range.

To test their ideas, the research team studied several hundred project teams in a medium-sized Midwestern R&D firm over a one-year period. They collected both prior network and demographic data on the employees that formed the teams and then assessed the teams' performances subsequently. They demonstrate statistically that demographic diversity is indeed both positively related to external network range and negatively related to internal network density. As a result, demographic diversity is not a consistent predictor of team performance.

Both internal network density and external network range, however, improve team performance. They conclude that both weak tie and strong tie social capital must be considered when managing team composition in work organizations.

EXTRAORGANIZATIONAL SOCIAL CAPITAL

3.3 Paying employees for referrals

In a path-breaking study, Fernandez, Castilla, and Moore (2001) provide empirical confirmation that investing in the social capital of employees can yield economic returns for firms. In their study, the social capital is in the employees' non-work networks, and the returns come through new employee referrals. This paper complements the work of Marsden and Gorman (1999). The latter studied internal staffing, whereas Fernandez and his colleagues studied external hiring.

Fernandez et al. began by positing three social mechanisms by which referrals occur and might provide value to the hiring firm: the richer pool, better match, and social enrichment mechanisms. We'll sketch the essential points of each in turn and then take a look at the evidence they found for each of these mechanisms in their study.

In the *richer pool* mechanism, referrals by current employees provide additional and *different applicants* than would be provided from non-referral sources (such as web postings, advertisements, job placement services, etc.) that are in fact more appropriate in terms of the job requirements, salary level, and so forth.

This greater appropriateness is attributed to two factors:

1. *Homophily* in human capital (skills, education, experience, etc.) between current employees and those they refer. If we accept that social relations are often homophilous (based on similarities), then by virtue of being in the employees' social networks they are similar to the current employees. If we also accept that the current employees are appropriate for their jobs, then those in their networks should also be appropriate.

2. The *reputation* motive, which posits that employees will pre-screen referrals so that those they refer are suitable in order to enhance their own reputation as valuable to their company. If an employee were to refer a friend who was a slacker, this might damage their own reputation directly (since they wasted managers' time) and by association (since they hang out with slackers).

The richer pool mechanism would provide economic value by reducing the number of screens (tests and interviews), and the associated cost. Screens are reduced primarily because fewer applicants need to be screened before a suitable hire is found.

In the misnamed *better match* mechanism, the key idea is that the referring employee provides a broadband information channel that would not exist with non-referred employees. This information channel provides additional information both to the applicant about the company and the nature of the job and, as a result, in the application itself. Hiring officials might also have more information (whether correct or not) if they infer homophily or use the referring employee as an indirect channel to ask for more details than they might have time for in a normal interview process. The information flow to the applicant might also have the effect of a realistic job preview.

The better match mechanism would provide economic value by bringing better timing and quality of application materials, higher acceptance rates, and lower turnover. All of these would reduce costs to the hiring firm, saving managerial time in reviewing ill-timed or incomplete applications, saving time and costs of waiting for a decision from the applicant, and saving the expense of a new search and training, respectively.

The *social enrichment* mechanism posits that a workplace which contains someone you already know in your non-work social network is both more friendly and a venue for mentoring to occur naturally. The new employee not only has someone whom they can ask questions they might worry would make them look dumb if they asked their supervisor, but has someone with whom to go on break or out to lunch. Friendship helps to prevent alienation.

A socially enriched work environment might lessen formal training and/ or turnover, bringing associated economic savings.

To provide evidence for their theories, Fernandez et al. studied the filling of entry level positions in the phone service center of a large bank with headquarters located in the San Francisco Bay area. Some facts about the setting include:

- 37 percent referrals-to-applicants ratio;
- interpersonal skills are important;
- on-the-job training is more critical than formal education; and
- regulations exist regarding breach of fiduciary trust.

If we review back to the job factors identified by Marsden and Gorman, we see that this setting is apt for social capital methods to work. They pointed to interpersonal skills, on-the-job training, and the need for legitimacy as key job factors for favoring social capital methods.

The results of this study demonstrated that referrals provide a richer pool, with:

- higher interview and offer rates;
- fewer overqualified, overpaid applicants;
- distinct background characteristics in terms of experience, skills, and career histories that represented homophily (between referrer and applicant) in gender and education, as well as wages and tenure at prior jobs;
- some evidence of better interpersonal skills.

There was no support for the better match mechanism, and limited support for the social enrichment mechanism. The latter was evident through interdependent turnover between applicant and referrer, although this interdependence did not lower turnover rates and so provided no savings. The primary – indeed sole – economic return to the company came through needing fewer screens for referral applicants versus non-referred applicants. This occurred because it took fewer referral applicants to find a suitable hire.

3.4   Managing the market interface

We can continue with our examination of the effects of the social capital of employees in their networks outside of the focal organization by turning to Broschak, who looks at it from the opposite frame of reference to that of Fernandez and his colleagues. Fernandez et al. considered how employees' extra-work networks could be used to bring new employees into the organization. Broschak (2004), by contrast, considers whether employees' extra-work ties impact what goes with them when they leave.

Broschak's thesis is that interfirm relationships, for example those among a buying firm and its suppliers, are socially embedded. *Social embeddedness* refers to the *multiplexity of relations that arises when relations governing economic exchange are built on or overlain by social ties.* In other words, not only do the firms exchange goods or services for payment or other consideration, but the actors who carry out these economic exchanges maintain friendship, advice, support, or other informal relationships.

Such embeddedness may occur because agents of the firms become friends as a result of their interacting on behalf of their organizations to carry out their duties (economic tie appropriated for social use). Or it may occur because agents influence their organizations to form economic partnerships with firms that employ their friends (social tie appropriated for economic use). For Broschak, how the economic relation becomes socially embedded is less important than the impact that such embeddedness has on the stability of the economic partnerships.

Broschak identifies three types of individual investments that exchange managers make that impact the stability of economic partnerships:

1. *Relationship-specific skills.* These refer to understanding how a particular partner likes to do business, and knowing 'private, tacit, and proprietary information' about the exchange partner (2004, p. 612). The former puts the exchange partner at ease, while the latter allows transactions to be conducted in shorthand, in a sense.
2. *Deep technical knowledge.* Exchange managers learn about the partner's business – in terms of their product and service offerings, as well as their production and administrative processes. As a result, the exchange manager can engage in joint problem solving with the partner firm, and offer ways to improve the partner's business that can benefit both firms.
3. *Personal relations.* These help to build trust, providing social capital to the firms in terms of obligations, information channels, and norms. This social capital helps, first, to minimize opportunism, second, to improve coordination, and, third, to ease conflict resolution.

As Broschak points out, 'the potential gains from these investments are high, while their value is lost outside of the exchange relationship' (2004, p. 612). Social capital is not fungible.

As a result, the exit of an exchange manager has a twin effect: lowering the value of the exchange relationship itself, while also reducing the costs associated with switching to another partner. Note that this is true for both partners. Thus we'd expect that the exit of an exchange manager at either partner would increase the likelihood that the interfirm partnership will dissolve.

Broschak tests this hypothesis using data on US advertising agencies and advertisers over a 12-year period in the 1980s and 1990s. This is an apt research setting for two reasons. First, advertising is a creative service that therefore relies on the human, as well as the social, capital of professionals at the firms, more so than on physical assets (e.g. plant, property, or equipment). Second, advertising is jointly produced by the agency and client firms. Thus 'relationships between exchange managers play an important role in producing advertising and maintaining client–agency relationships' (2004, p. 616).

Some facts on the industry include the number and duration of such partnerships for agencies and clients. On average, clients partner with three agencies per year and dissolve one such interfirm tie every other year. The average duration of clients' ties with their agencies is approximately seven years. Agencies, by contrast, partner with roughly 20 clients per year, on average, of which four dissolve each year. Agencies average keeping clients for about five years.

Statistical analyses support the social capital hypothesis, but with some contingencies. Economic partnerships are indeed more likely to dissolve subsequent to the exit of an exchange manager, whether that manager was on the agency or the client side. For clients, the effect of managers' mobility varies with firm size, being greatest for larger firms. For agencies, the effect of exchange managers' mobility was conditional on the number of economic partnerships the agency maintains, with social and human capital changes being less disruptive for agencies with many market ties.

3.5   Exploiting reputational capital

Recall that norms are the standards or expectations of behavior that are shared by a collective. Put in the context of social capital, Arnold and Kay's (1999) study highlights the impact that weak tie social capital outside of a firm can have on the development of strong tie social capital within the firm.

Arnold and Kay are concerned with the standards of behavior that are written into codes of conduct, or ethics, for members of a profession. They note that social structure should, on one hand, put pressure on individuals to abide by codes of conduct and, on the other hand, also provide a buffer which shields violators from detection. Recall the conspiracy study of Baker and Faulkner (1993). Since social capital is, as Coleman (1988) told us, a public good that exists in social relations, they argue that larger firms potentially provide more global social capital as a public good into which individual members can tap.

They take as their research setting the legal profession. Here is their theory in brief. Large law firms start owing to an excess of social capital. The dynamic is that a good lawyer gains clients through word-of-mouth referrals by current and past clients. This employs the social networks of clients to build a reputation. At some point, there are too many referrals for one lawyer to handle all the cases. Thus our reputed lawyer takes on a partner, and so on until the firm becomes large. Note that the lawyer needed human capital to be good enough to handle the initial cases well. It is not an excess of human capital that leads to the circumstance where there is too much business to handle. An excess of human capital would produce the opposite result, as the lawyer would be capable of handling more and more cases without the need to expand. Instead, it is the reputation, a marker of social capital, that prompts law firms to grow in size.

According to Arnold and Kay (1999), this social capital not only brings value in terms of new clients, but also brings value in terms of the clients' perceptions. The status of the firm shapes the way clients interpret the conduct of the lawyers, being more likely to give high status firms the benefit of the doubt that any behavior that seems questionable is either not so – since the firm is above questioning – or is an innocent mistake.

The need to protect this reputational resource, a form of weak tie social capital outside of the firm, prompts the development of strong tie social capital inside the firm. This internal social capital is manifested in:

- *intense socialization*, as each new lawyer brought on board learns what is expected from other members of the firm, both in training and by having tenured members acting as role models; and
- *mutual oversight*, in which lawyers remind each other of what is expected and catch possible misconduct or any behavior that might be so construed, even if it is an innocent mistake, before it has negative consequences.

These processes lead large law firms specifically to have more normative social capital available to individual lawyers within firms.

Arnold and Kay (1999) present evidence in a study of Canadian law firms. They find that sole practitioners:

- receive a disproportionate amount of complaints of misconduct;
- receive disproportionately more serious complaints;
- participate disproportionately in violations of higher levels of trust;
- receive disproportionately more sanctions.

On the other hand, lawyers in large firms receive disproportionately fewer and less severe complaints, and fewer sanctions.

Generalizing these findings, the implication for human resource managers comes in understanding the norm-building processes that operate through the social structure of the firm. Socialization, in which tenured employees introduce newcomers to expected behaviors, and oversight, in which employees watch each other's backs, can be managed for the benefit of the firm, as in the case of the Canadian law firms. These processes could work to the firm's detriment, with norms undermining the organization's goals. Social network analysis can aid the HR manager in making sure the social structure supports a firm's attainment of goals and does not protect an internal conspiracy.

We have seen that managing social capital can benefit organizations in a number of ways, in filling internal vacancies, in recruiting new employees, in managing market relationships, and in shaping the larger environment. In the next chapter, we'll discuss how social capital can benefit members of organizations, and how individuals can manage their social capital.

4 Egocentric concepts and applications

Our next goal is to apply the basic concepts of social capital by taking the perspective of individuals, asking how they (or you) can use social capital to get ahead. We will be concerned with learning when to use social capital, both weak and strong, as well as with how to enact the interactions through which social capital gets developed and exchanged.

4.1 Perceptions and promotions

Dan Brass conducted some of the earlier studies of how individuals' social networks impact their influence and chances of promotion in work organizations. Brass (1984) is one of the first studies to separate three kinds of social relations that are roughly equivalent to Krackhardt and Hansen's (1993) notions of communication, advice, and trust. Brass measured employees' communication, workflow (similar here to advice, although elsewhere we will use the term workflow to indicate the formal flow of work), and friendship (inferred to indicate trust) ties. In addition to measuring different types of networks, Brass looked at variation in job categories (being in the technical core as against being in supportive functions) and workgroups (such as departments or teams).

Brass found the following:

- *Strong, cohesive ties* outside of one's workgroup, particularly to what he terms the dominant coalition of the organization, *increase perceptions of influence*. The dominant coalition is the group of workers with the most influence. An effect of strong ties on influence exists for all workers, but strong ties are especially impactful for workers in the technical core, who are unable to attain any influence without such ties. It's also true that the more critical your job function, the more influence you have, so that both informal networks and aspects of the formal organization are important. This latter finding helps to explain why social ties are so important for workers in the technical core. The contribution of each individual is less critical for such workers, as there are many of them (versus, say, fewer managers).
- *Weak, bridging ties*, particularly within one's department (but not exclusively so), are *needed for promotions*. This finding is equally true for all workers, both in the technical core and in administrative or support roles.

Flap and Boxman (1999) studied managers in Dutch companies to see whether arguments about weak tie social capital would hold up in describing how workers found better managerial, rather than entry level, positions and reaped greater income within those ranks.

To begin, they concluded from their study that those who found their managerial position using informal, or social, ties, as opposed to job advertisements or placement services, reported:

- decreased search costs;
- better jobs (greater income, responsibility, and satisfaction);
- higher returns once on the job (in terms of income).

They also observed that social ties are used disproportionately more often for filling managerial jobs at higher levels of rank and responsibility.

These findings are very consistent with those of Granovetter and Burt. However, Flap and Boxman also recorded tie strength, based on self-reports from respondents, cross-checked whenever possible. They found that weak ties carry more new *information*, and are thus used much more frequently overall in getting a job as a manager than are strong ties, but strong ties engender *trust* and, while rare, they are disproportionately used to get managerial jobs at the highest levels. Once on the job, they observe a similar distinction:

- Weak ties are especially important to those in lower managerial positions for moving up.
- Strong ties are especially useful for those in higher level positions for entering the executive team.

To fully reconcile these findings we need the ideas not only of Granovetter and Burt, but also of Coleman (1988). Recall that Coleman predicted that strong ties set the social stage for the development of trust. Strong tie social structures provide advantages for mobilizing resources at the community level, or where the good of the overall organization is at stake, rather than just the fortunes of particular individuals in competition with one another. With regard to work organizations, the application of Coleman's ideas about strong ties is advanced by the work of Eva Meyerson (1999).

Meyerson reasons that, because cohesion engenders trust and enables the mobilization of resources, strong ties within an organization are needed to reach the highest levels and increase incomes for managers at the executive team level. In her study, the triads were allowed to include outside contacts. She makes two key observations for why trust, and hence strong ties, is so important in breaking into the executive team:

1. The *higher up* a position is located in the organization, the stronger the impact the individual has on the performance and *survival* of the organization.
2. The higher up a position, the more *difficult* it is to specify formal selection and compensation rules.

The existence or nonexistence of formal criteria for selection and compensation seems important. Burt (2000) underscored this in studies in which he found that female managers and males who have just entered the upper echelons needed strong ties to get further promotions. Established male executives at an investment bank (where formal criteria may be more readily available) benefited, in terms of larger bonuses, from weak, bridging ties.

4.2   Personality matters

The above findings paint a general picture of how different social positions provide differential benefits to those within a social structure. Aside from a minor point on gender differences, the theories are supposed to hold for the average actor. Of course, the average person is a statistical fiction, so it is worth asking: Who benefits from what kind of social capital?

We can surmise, from the process of homophily and our knowledge of the demographic make-up of organizations, that factors such as gender, race, ethnicity, age, and socioeconomic status should impact the extent to which actors can 1) find themselves in an advantageous position within the social structure of an organization and 2) actually reap the benefits of their social position.

Traditionally, as an example, we would find upper-class, middle-aged, white males to be most likely to form strong ties to members of the upper echelons of large corporations – just the kind of ties needed if people are to have influence and advance into executive positions within such firms and reap the attendant benefits.

Mehra, Kilduff, and Brass (2001) seek to push our understanding beyond the obvious and overt demographics. They examine how different personality types not only benefit from social networks but also create the social structures that benefit some and constrain others. The personality variable they measure is called self-monitoring.

Self-monitoring, in general, refers to the willingness and ability of persons to 'monitor and control their self expressions in social situations' (Mehra et al., 2001, p. 124). Individuals can be classified as either high or low self-monitoring.

High self-monitors act 'with chameleon like ease, they present the right image to the right audience' (p. 124). They read social cues, in the behavior or expressions of others, and use these cues to tailor their own behavior and expression. They are likely to feel at ease with compromise and thus tend to emerge as leaders in collaborative work environments.

Low self-monitors, by contrast, 'insist on being themselves, no matter how incongruent their self expression may be with the requirements of the social situation' (p. 124). They base their behavior and expression on their own underlying attitudes and emotions. They are true, quoting Mehra et al., in turn quoting Shakespeare, 'to thine own self'.

Mehra and his colleagues offer three models by which self-monitoring may predict how network position influences workplace performance and promotion: the mediation model, the interaction model, and the additive model.

1. In the *mediation* model, self-monitoring enables actors to obtain advantageous positions in the social structure, which then influences performance in the ways we have already studied. That is, where a person is in the informal network of the organization is what determines the outcomes (promotion, compensation) they receive, but those high in self-monitoring are more likely to find themselves in advantageous positions.

2. The *interaction* model specifies that self-monitoring allows actors to get the most from their position in the social structure. In this model, both high and low self-monitors may find themselves similarly situated in the informal networks of an organization, but only the high self-monitors will be able to take advantage of their social position.

3. The *additive* model, lastly, specifies that self-monitoring has independent effects on performance, but does not play a role in how network position influences outcomes. Both high and low self-monitors may find themselves similarly positioned in the informal network of their organization, and both may garner benefits from their social ties, but high self-monitors will outcompete low self-monitors for outcomes based on the additional benefits of their personality type in modern work organizations.

Mehra et al. tested these theoretical models using data from a small (approximately 100 employees) high-technology firm in the Southeast portion of the United States. Their findings showed support for both the mediation and the additive models and point to a 'complex relationship among self-monitoring, structural position, and performance' (2001, p. 138). High self-monitors used their experience in the organization to navigate into network positions that tapped into more weak tie social capital, by bridging otherwise unconnected others. This structural position paid off in higher performance ratings, leading in turn to valued outcomes. But high self-monitors also outperformed low self-monitors above and beyond the differences due to the weak tie social capital in the networks of the high self-monitors.

It's worth noting that Mehra et al.'s study did not provide any evidence of differences in the strong tie social capital of high and low self-monitors, but neither did they find any relationship between strong tie social capital and performance. This may have been due to the particularities of their study, which used only one personality variable and gave only a snapshot of a small firm with a stable managerial team.

4.3   Navigating social exchange

Whether you are a high or a low self-monitor, navigating the social landscape clearly has important implications for your career development. Social interactions in the workplace can frequently be viewed as negotiations, as each party seeks to gain or offer information, resources, or support. McGinn and Keros (2002) explore how such negotiations work in weak (or arm's length) versus strong (or close) ties.

To begin, they observed numerous dyadic social interactions and identified three so-called *logics of exchange* that governed behaviors during the incidence of contact:

1. full, *mutual* honesty;
2. *cooperative* problem solving;
3. head-to-head *competition*.

In most cases, the actors quickly settled into one of these logics and then improvised behaviors accordingly: opening up when the logic was mutualistic, working together when the logic was cooperative, and haggling when the logic was competitive.

To highlight the differences between the three logics, let's translate them into a negotiation over the sale and purchase of a new car:

- In the *mutualistic* logic, the dealer would be open about the actual costs to them of all aspects relating to the vehicle, along with any special incentives they may get from the factory or a dealer's association. The buyer would be honest about what they are willing and able to pay.
- In the *cooperative* logic, neither party would disclose their bottom lines, so to speak, but each would make reasonable offers and counteroffers, while acknowledging the other's interests. So, the buyer would seek to allow the dealer a fair profit and the dealer would seek to give the buyer a good deal.

- In the *competitive* logic, the dealer would try to persuade the buyer to pay full price, or even more, perhaps by noting how quickly that model sells, while the buyer would try to get the lowest price, regardless of whether the dealer is forced to take a loss.

McGinn and Keros found that stronger ties promoted a more mutualistic logic, characterized by opening up on both sides, and leading to an agreement and successful exchange. Weaker ties were more likely to lead to a cooperative logic, with problem-solving behaviors leading to successful exchange agreements. Lastly, the pattern was complete in that strangers, with no ties, accounted for successful, agreed-upon exchanges based on the competitive, haggling behaviors. Note that the logic of exchange plays a strong role in mediating a successful exchange based on the type of social ties. It was, in their study, not uncommon for complete strangers to open up, but in none of these cases was the exchange successfully agreed on and completed.

In some cases, a common logic was not coordinated, and the nature of the exchange was then asymmetric, in the sense that each party followed a different logic. Only one of these cases occurred among parties with social ties, and an agreement was not reached. Between strangers, agreements were possible in spite of the asymmetric understanding of what had taken place. In essence, one party took advantage of the other, who remained oblivious.

In other cases, a common logic was not settled on quickly, but was worked out as a result of one of three tactics identified by McGinn and Keros: process clarification, trust testing, and emotional punctuation.

In *process clarification*, one or both parties explicitly question the rules of interaction. For instance, you might expressly ask them why they are not opening up or seeing things from your side. Among those with social ties, such process clarifications broke competitive logics and replaced them with cooperative ones. Among strangers, however, the reverse occurred: attempts to clarify the process as cooperative were rebuffed, and the ending logic was competitive.

Trust testing, in which one party makes a move that leaves them vulnerable in order to signal a willingness to cooperate, and *emotional punctuations*, involving outbursts of humor, anger, or frustration, were sometimes used successfully by strangers in transitioning competitive initial logics into cooperative ones. These tactics were not always successful, however, and led at other times to asymmetric ending logics.

4.4 Social capital and having a mentor
Studies about mentoring relationships and the value that they can have for newcomers in organizations have suggested that having a mentor early in

your career can provide many benefits. Some of the potential benefits can be framed in terms of social capital. These social capital-related benefits of mentoring can be broadly classified into two categories: *career help* and *psychosocial help*.

Career help consists of such activities as *sponsoring, exposure, coaching, challenge, and protection*. Career help typically constitutes the focus during the earliest career stage of initiation, which occurs during the first 6–12 months on the job.

- Sponsoring is the provision of resources needed for a particular task or goal.
- Exposure involves providing a reason for being at important meetings, lunches, and so on with those outside of the employee's immediate workflow.
- Coaching is providing specific help in performing tasks.
- Challenge comes through getting assignments that can prove an employee's skills and worth.
- Protection means keeping the employee from unattractive assignments, such as doing 'grunt' work.

Psychosocial help consists of activities like *role modeling, counseling, acceptance, confirmation, and friendship*. Psychosocial help complements career help during the cultivation stage which follows initiation, occurring over the subsequent two to five years.

- Role models exhibit expected behaviors outside of job duties, such as dress, language, and so on.
- Counselors help an employee work through personal issues.
- Acceptance and confirmation provide a sense of affiliation and belongingness as well as validation.
- Friendship makes the workplace less alienating.

Now, without denying the many other benefits of mentoring, what Higgins and Nohria (1999) want us to consider is that obtaining early career help from a mentor may bring social capital-related liabilities instead of benefits. To explain their idea, they group the social capital-related activities of career help into three categories that they call mechanisms: signaling, access, and opportunities.

- *Signaling* refers to demonstrating your worth to the organization, by virtue of the mentor being willing to invest their time and energy in helping you and your career. Since the mentor is typically a high level person to whom 'time is money', you must be worth some money for them to invest their time, or so goes the positive spin on this mechanism. The mentor also introduces you to the upper echelon, or dominant coalition in Brass's (1984) terms, which increases your perceived influence. There is selection prestige, similar to being a first-round draft pick in professional sports. Owing to this prestige, others may want to get to know you. Lastly, there is a signal that you have a role in helping the mentor in their successful endeavors. In some sense, you may get to 'ride the coat-tails' of your mentor: their successes become your successes.

- *Access* refers to the direct channel for information and resources that you possess through your mentor. Mentors are often in a formal position where they have access to information and control over resources that they can provide to you. They are also typically well connected in the social structure, and can in some sense lend you their social capital. Rather than having to seek out and develop a relationship with a person who has the information you need, you go to your mentor, who already has a tie to a suitable other, and your mentor finds out what you need to know.

- *Opportunities* refers to the ability of a high level mentor to control who gets the best assignments. This occurs because mentors are often in positions with hiring or personnel allocation authority. By best assignments, we mean those that will allow you to make the best use of your human capital and that are highly visible and important to the organization, allowing you to be in line for compensation and promotion if things go well.

We have explained the three mechanisms by referring to their potential benefits. Higgins and Nohria (1999) see possible liabilities lurking in each mechanism.

For signaling, they suggest that having a powerful mentor could reduce others' motivation to seek you out to develop relationships, for fear of stepping on your mentor's toes. That is, why should they try to help you out when you have a mentor who can do it and to some extent whose job it is to help you out? The signal of your value may be intimidating. They may worry that you would feel superior to them or that it may not be safe to confide in you because of your relationship to a senior-ranking person. In contrast to your getting some credit for the successes of your mentor, the negative converse would be that you do not get credit for your own successes – instead they are attributed to your mentor.

The access provided by a mentor may be a liability when it comes to developing social capital, because it may reduce your own motivation to seek out ties to others beyond your mentor. Social ties involve time and energy; why expend them when you have your mentor and his or her social capital to draw on when you need help in learning your job or finding out what is going on in the organization?

Opportunities have a potential downside when a mentor can get you interesting and high-profile assignments, and protect you from grunt work. If it happens too early in your career and before you and your mentor have a psychosocial relationship, your mentor may be a bit too eager and place you on assignments that you are not ready to handle. This can lead to initial failure that can undermine your sense of self-efficacy and competence. After all, if you can't handle the first assignment you are given, you might wonder whether you've chosen the right career!

There are three points to keep in mind:

1.   These are potential liabilities. Higgins and Nohria are not claiming that mentoring is necessarily bad.
2.   These are liabilities for developing your subsequent social capital. Other benefits, not related to social capital, may outweigh these concerns.
3.   These are liabilities associated with getting career help too early.

Higgins and Nohria do not discuss any potential liabilities associated with either psychosocial help or later career help. Indeed, their study suggests that both are valuable. Hence, we are talking about potential liabilities in terms of developing your other social ties or getting career help from a mentor too early (particularly before you develop a psychosocial relationship with the mentor).

Their evidence underscores the last point. They studied 323 male upper-middle level managers of a multinational corporation (MNC) in consumer electronics. They asked each respondent whether he had a mentoring relationship early on and also whether he had one later in his tenure with the company. These were not necessarily formally assigned mentors. Then they assessed social capital by counting the number of bridging ties each respondent had, where a bridging tie is to a person in another division of the company.

The results showed the following:

● Early career mentoring *decreases* by 60 percent the odds of subsequently having more weak tie social capital. That is, if you have a mentor in the first 6–12 months who provides any of the career help functions discussed above, then you are only (a little more than) half as likely to develop a wide social network when compared to someone who does not receive early career mentoring.

- Later career mentoring *increases* by 380 percent the odds of subsequently having more weak tie social capital. That is, if you have a mentor after your first year or two on the job who provides any of the career help functions, then you are almost four times more likely to have a wide social network when compared to someone who does not receive later career mentoring.

As a result, speaking again of career help, we can say that if you do not have a mentor early on in your tenure with a company, but then pick one up later, you will have the widest social network. Your social network will be the narrowest if you have a mentor initially but not later.

By investigating the career paths of those who did not have early mentors, Higgins and Nohria also concluded that early formal training facilitates the development of subsequent social capital by providing a venue for social interaction and the development of natural later mentoring. In other words, if employees have formal training programs to rely on for career help, they can focus on the psychosocial support aspects of their interpersonal relationships, which can then evolve into later career help mentoring.

4.5 Negative social relations

For Higgins and Nohria (1999), the liabilities that resulted from early career help mentoring were an unintended consequence of what was otherwise assumed to be a positive relationship. The mentor and sidekick were assumed to like one another and be working toward the common goal of fostering the sidekick's career development. Brass and Labianca (1999) are concerned with liabilities that result from social relations where the parties are not so positively inclined.

They begin with a definition: A negative social relation exists when at least one party has a negative *affective* judgment about the other. They note that every relation has positive and negative aspects, because there are always costs (in time, energy, and emotional investment) as well as benefits, but such costs are an investment, not a liability. Instead, they note that a global, affective judgment is also formed by each party about the other. A global, affective judgment is simply a determination of whether one likes someone else, on balance. Negative social ties cannot always be avoided, especially in a work setting. You can choose your friends, but not all your co-workers (likewise, not all your relatives, so this is not just about work).

Their main point is that all the benefits of social capital can turn to liabilities when a person is involved in a negative social tie. They would experience less recruitment and selection, slower promotions, less compensation, lower satisfaction, less influence, and impaired career development. Clearly, if a person had many negative ties and few positive ones, we would expect such dire consequences. Is there reason to worry about a negative tie or two if you have many positive ones? Brass and Labianca think so.

Drawing on social-psychological theories of negative asymmetry, they predict that negative ties have substantial impact, and a single negative tie may outweigh many positive ties – negating the benefits you might otherwise garner from your social capital.

There are two main reasons for negative asymmetry:

- *Contrast effects.* Negative ties are less frequent and so they stand out and capture our attention. Since we do not expect to see negative ties, they may capture our attention and thus receive undue weight when we are evaluating a person for compensation or promotion. For instance, if we received a negative letter of reference for a candidate, we might be unlikely to hire them even if they also have more positive letters than any other candidate.
- *Lack of ambiguity.* We tend to have more gradated positive feelings, but more definite negative ones. We often temper our positive recommendations with terms like 'pretty good', 'not bad', and so forth, but we use stronger terms for negative evaluations.

Other than the potential for negative asymmetry, social liabilities are influenced by the same factors as social capital:

- the *network structure*, including density, closure, and multiplexity;
- the *formal organization*, including the prescribed workflow, physical proximity, and size;
- your *human capital*, including education, experience, attributes, and attitudes.

4.6   Tokenism

We have repeatedly seen that homophily is something of a basic principle and process in social networks. When ties occur informally, they tend to form on the basis of some commonality, be it an interest, an experience, or simple proximity in physical space. Often, demographic characteristics – race, gender, and so on – serve as proxies for other commonalities and so are often observed as drivers of homophily. It's worth noting, since it plays in nicely in a moment, that such demographics often correlate with status, particularly in settings where there is a predominant majority class, such as men in corporate top management.

Louise Roth (2004) argues that homophily preferences combine with status expectations to produce the phenomenon known as tokenism. In other words, she sees a dark side when social capital is allowed to take its natural course. Tokenism can limit opportunities to exploit one's human capital as well as shape how performance utilization of human capital is evaluated. When one demographic class is in the numerical minority and of lower status it is thus disadvantaged by the social structure. Let's review her theory for just how tokenism results from the two cognitive processes identified: *homophily preferences* are the primary mechanism leading to tokenism, while *status expectations* determine how tokenism is experienced.

First, tokens are defined as members of a small minority in a field that is otherwise predominated by a single, majority demographic class. Here the example is women on Wall Street. She reviews three common experiences that constitute tokenism:

1.   heightened visibility, escalating performance pressure;
2.   isolation from informal social networks, heightening boundaries;
3.   role encapsulation, forcing enactment of stereotypical scripts.

The effects of tokenism are not uniform, however. Instead, they are contingent on status. Female tokens in male-dominated fields typically suffer as a result of their experiences as tokens. Men in female-dominated areas, by contrast, often reap benefits. As Roth states: 'This [result] suggests that the consequences of tokenism depend on the relative status of the tokens compared to the majority' (2004, p. 192). Homophily preferences and status expectations explain why.

We already know about homophily preferences, but we'll let Roth remind us: 'Homophily preferences are a tendency for people to prefer to associate with others who are like themselves' (2004, p. 192). She points out that this can happen almost 'automatically and unconsciously'. The result, regardless of intention, is that strict homophily preferences will lead to an informal social structure in which the minority is broken off in a small component, disjoint from the majority component. Such isolation and a heightened sense of visibility and contrast are features of tokenism.

Status expectations are 'beliefs about the superiority of some people over others in relation to some task' (2004, p. 193). That may be a bit too strong a way of putting it, but the point is right. We assume people of higher status have more human capital, and thus can perform better at many tasks, particularly higher level or more valuable ones. Often, of course, the assumption is correct, for instance when status comes from education or experience. But status often comes from demographic characteristics, such as race or gender, which are not task relevant. They are, nonetheless, what are referred to as diffuse status characteristics, meaning they are:

- readily apparent;
- salient; and
- determinant.

That is, we rely upon them to understand others, ascribing behavior to the characteristic rather than other factors. The upshot is that we also expect others to rely upon our understanding of them when they interact with us. The combination of status expectations across categories of a diffuse status characteristic puts pressure on low status tokens to perform in accordance with the expectation held by the high status majority while simultaneously prejudicing evaluation.

To break out of this dark hole of tokenism, Roth argues in favor of developing both social capital and human capital in the forms of strong mentors and specialized skill sets. Mentorship is, in fact, a mechanism by which homophily preferences operate to perpetuate discrepancies in opportunities. Heterophilous mentors, in theory, can offset some of the impact.

Specialized skill sets are a more robust strategy for countering tokenism. First, they change the nature of role encapsulation and take advantage of heightened visibility. They can also, for critical skills, shape informal networks, as men who otherwise would go to other men for assistance no longer have that option. In other words, the preference for homophily cannot be sustained, and social capital is garnered from the resulting interactions.

Evidence: Roth constructed career histories for 76 new MBAs from 'five elite graduate programs' who entered Wall Street in the 1990s. While men outnumber women 5:1 in the population, her sample comprised 44 women and 32 men. She found that women were disproportionately subject to stereotyping and harassment, while shut out of access to important client accounts and social networks. Through in-depth interviews, she traced the origins to homophily preferences, which 'had the effect of reducing affinities with co-workers and managers for employees in the minority' (2004, p. 198).

4.7   Status, ascription, and expectation

Koput and Gutek (in press), echoing Burt (2001), note that the maintenance of positive affect in a close relationship can be paramount in any informational role. From an informational standpoint, strong ties have often been seen as bigger pipes, able to transmit more, and richer, information. Yet, following Burt, if one assumes that close friends have similar primary sources of information, there's not much benefit to derive. That is, there would seem to be little value to a broader bandwidth in transmitting information that one already possesses. But there may be some benefit, just not in novel information. Instead, the benefit may be to reinforce beliefs and give more confidence to actions. In short, close ties serve to emotionally support, rather than to influence the direction of, decisions.

Koput and Gutek argue that status determines whether cohesion provides a broader bandwidth or creates an echo chamber. High status alters may cling to the rules of etiquette particularly in dealing with low status egos. When a low status ego has views that are not widely shared, high status alters may not see it as their role to provide critical information. This is especially true in cases where status runs along the line of gender, as sex roles may interfere with men's candor.

Recall that, when actors are not established, they are subject to status expectations, ascriptive tendencies based on diffuse status characteristics such as gender. Since preferences for homophily generate tokenism, and social isolation further heightens boundaries, cohesive cross-gender ties would seem to be a sensible prescription to establish legitimacy and reduce sex-based ascription. The logic here follows Meyerson (1999) in that stronger ties, with their closure and multiple connections, provide trust, which serves in place of more specifiable measures of performance. A person is no longer a caricatured representative of a caste, but a complex individual and member of the community. Ascribed causes are untenable when ties provide higher-quality information on which to base judgments. Put differently, legitimacy is a buffer from ascription, signaling that some women are not subject to homophilous preferences or status expectations.

In the absence of legitimacy, low status members cannot engage in high status activities without going noticed, particularly when their status is made salient by the spilling over of other factors, such as:

- *Attitudinal sex role spillover* (perceptions of exclusion or differential treatment). This makes women vulnerable owing to a lowering of their own expectations for inclusion and aspirations from encounters. Women who expect exclusion may pre-emptively curtail their behavior – self-handicap to avoid confronting the stereotype. To the extent this is in keeping with homophilous preferences or status expectations, such behavior risks increasing ascription. Feelings of exclusion or biased treatment will be reinforced and cemented with a false sense of certainty.

- *Sex-typed outside roles.* Women who occupy roles associated with being female, such as wife, mother, receptionist, sex object, and so on become more vulnerable to ascription owing to the increased salience of stereotypes those roles bring. The spilling over of sex roles from outside the organization results in the cuing of status expectations within the workplace. The information and experiences from sex-typed outside life roles induce selective sharing of information from alters to ego, which reinforces the roles and further encapsulates ego as lower status.

- *Counter-type roles.* Women who occupy valued social roles, such as in the leadership ranks, not only violate role encapsulation, but they make themselves more visible and thus more prone to ascription owing to homophilous preferences and status expectations. Etiquette requires pro forma interaction with those in visible, valued positions. This increases the likelihood and strength of ties existing from high status alters to a low status ego, while making the interactions less critically informative.

Koput and Gutek collected data at multiple points in time on demographics, social interactions, leadership, retention, and placement for five cohorts of undergraduate students at a large Southwestern university over the last two years of their academic program and through the job search process. They examined pre-hire mechanisms underlying retention and placement, along with the concomitant variables of leadership, commitment, and satisfaction, as outcomes among our student population.

Let's quickly recap their findings. The interplay between social ties and sex role spillover is complex, but the key results can be summarized in a few points.

For women with low salience of sex role spillover, cohesion to men improves behavioral outcomes and allows such women to occupy valued roles, but hurts women's commitment and satisfaction. Non-cohesive contacts to other women improve retention, but hinder placement. Cohesion in ties to women offsets the positive effect of those ties for retention, but makes those same gender ties less of an impediment to placement.

For women with high salience of sex role spillover, male cohesion is detrimental to their retention and placement, and the damaging effect on attitudes is amplified. Women who score high in attitudinal sex role spillover, have a number of sex-typed outside roles, and seek global leadership positions find that cohesion to women improves retention and attitudes while male contacts lacking cohesion help placement.

The above material is actually rather advanced for an introductory text, so we will end our theoretical review here. We have covered a lot of ground, including some basic ideas and steps in applying network analysis to organizations, the central concepts of social capital, and a number of ideas and applications to human resources and business management at both the organizational and the individual levels. Before proceeding to the methods of network analysis, some review is in order.

PART II

DATA METHODS

In this part, we introduce the techniques for how to obtain, prepare, and process both individual and relational data. Analyses of structure, position, and formation will follow, once the data is ready.

5 Obtaining data

In this chapter, we discuss how to obtain data.

As noted in Chapter 1, we collect the relational data by conducting a network survey. By this, we mean a population survey distributed to each and every member of the group or organization. The key here is that we need to ask each member to report their own social relations. Personal observation, in which we watch interactions, or interviewing one person, such as a boss, or a few members is subject to biases. By personally observing, we introduce our-selves into the social structure, and that may well alter interaction patterns. Interviewing the boss, for example, typically provides a structure skewed to look like what the formal structure is supposed to look like, rather than representing the actual social structure.

The first step in conducting any survey is to construct the survey instrument. Doing so entails writing questions and presenting them in a suitable format.

5.1 Relational data: survey construction

There are four principles to constructing the questions for a network survey to obtain data on informal, social relations in a formal group or organization: content, context, confidentiality, and convenience. These describe what you need to know or consider in developing your instrument.

5.1.a Content

By this, we mean the content of exchange or activity in the relations. Recall that we also referred to this as the type of social tie. Following Krackhardt and Hanson (1993), this may appear straightforward, as they gave us three types of ties to use. If we want to diagnose the informal organization at work, we can establish contents as communication, advice, and trust.

But it is not always so easy as just asking members of a particular group who they communicate with, who they seek advice from, and who they trust. This is because groups vary in the nature and degree of communication, trust, and advice, and because individuals may interpret these concepts differently even within a group. For each type of tie, we want to be as specific in defining the relation as possible.

For instance, rather than asking 'Who do you communicate with?', it would be preferable to define the particular modes of communication we are interested in, such as talking, emailing, and so on. In some groups, emails might be pro forma sent out on distribution lists. If so, we might prefer to ask just who they talk to face to face. But, even then, everyone in the group might talk to everyone else at some point or to some degree, so we may want specifically to ask who they talk to frequently. And, even then, 'frequently' is open to interpretation, so it would be better to specify a particular frequency for them, such as 'With whom do you talk typically every day?'

To use communication, trust, and advice as content to diagnose organizations, we want to establish work-related networks. So, rather than simply asking who they talk with, we'd rather ask 'With whom do you talk about work, typically every day?' And, of course, we need to separate advice from 'what's happening'. Hence, it is better to specify the content as just that: 'With whom do you talk about what's happening at work, typically every day?' Yet this may be too colloquial or abstract; if taken literally, we are asking who they talk to about anything at all. What a conundrum!

We can grapple with this task of survey instrument construction if we keep in mind that it is best to write questions that have three properties:

1. *Specificity.* Be as concrete and specific as possible. Avoid generic terms or abstract concepts.
2. *Behavioral anchors.* Ask about actual behaviors that the members of the group engage in on a regular basis, rather than hypothetical situations, attitudes, or perceptions.
3. *Proper directionality.* This requires some explanation. Social relations can occur in either a directed or an undirected way. Directed relations are those in which the relation is asymmetric, that is, it is not the same for the two parties. For instance, in work-related advice ties, one party is typically the expert and the other the novice. The novice goes to the expert for advice, and the expert gives advice to the novice, but these are different things. The expert does not go to the novice for advice just because the novice comes to them. So, it matters who is going to whom, and there is a distinct feature: these ties occur when one party seeks out the other to initiate the incidence of contact or exchange, for information, resources, support, or whatever. Undirected ties, by contrast, are symmetric and must be mutual. That is, one party cannot have the relation to the other without the other party having the same relation with the first. If I go to lunch with a colleague, I cannot do so unless the colleague goes to lunch with me. We have lunch together. Having lunch is therefore undirected. Note, of course, that paying for lunch is a different thing altogether. So is asking to lunch, which could be directed or undirected. One way to determine whether a relation is directed or

undirected is, as noted above, to see how the relation actually occurs. If one party seeks out the other to initiate the incidence of contact or exchange, it is directed. Undirected relations, by contrast, occur typically as byproducts of other interaction: we run into each other at the copier and chat about a variety of things, including what's happening at work. Then we would say we talk with each other and have an undirected communication tie.

So, with these properties in mind, a good example might be: 'Who do you talk to about the schedule of upcoming meetings at least once a week?' Good for a communication question. An advice example might be: 'Who do you go to at least once a month for help in filling out an audit worksheet?' Specific and behavioral for a public accounting firm, anyway. We'd have to substitute another example for 'filling out an audit worksheet' if we have a different organization.

I'm guessing you can infer the lesson here: writing the questions requires thought and care. Establishing the proper way to define content depends on the context, to which we now turn.

5.1.b   Context

Every group has, to some extent, its own language and culture. You want to know whether pairs of individuals are involved in various types of relations, but the specific activities that constitute each of these types of relations may vary from one group to another, both in form and in frequency.

For example, in one office they may have weekly meetings, so that asking who talks to whom at least once a week will not really discriminate communication patterns but rather pick up formal interaction. So you might ask about daily interaction, or you might specify 'outside of meetings'. In another office, it may be common for everyone to engage in small talk on a daily basis. If so, you'll want to ask not just about who talks with whom, but who talks with whom about important matters, being sure to provide a specific instance of an important behavior that actually occurs for members of the group. To get at advice, you may need to ask who goes to whom for technical information, or help in getting their job done, rather than use the term 'advice', which may be interpreted to mean personal, rather than job related. To get at trust, you may need to ask about support on unpopular matters, or who members go to when faced with a confidential matter. Or you might get at trust by asking about both friendship and work-related ties (using multiplexity to infer trust).

To find out what language is used to capture communication, trust, and advice, as we intend them (or whatever relations define your content), and how these relations occur (directionality), you should start off by doing a few things:

1. Interview some of the members of the group. Run sample questions past them and ask them how they would interpret each. Also ask them about the norms for frequency of informal interaction, as well as about formal interaction, such as meetings.
2. You might also observe the group at work or even work with the group as a member for some period.
3. Write a short pilot survey and give it to a few members of the group. Then carefully scrutinize their responses and confirm their accuracy for the content you are after. Adapt your questions accordingly.
4. Understand the formal roles and workflow of the organization or group. Definitely get a copy of the organization chart. As we've learned, to diagnose social capital we need to be able to compare the formal organization with the informal networks.

5.1.c   Confidentiality

Respondents must believe that their responses will be treated confidentially and that they will be used only to benefit themselves or their organization as a whole. Respondents must be assured that their responses will not be used to do them any harm. Respondents may want their identities to be protected.

Typically, we begin with an introductory statement assuring confidentiality, such as:

> As part of a class exercise at the University of Arizona, we are collecting data on the patterns of interaction among individuals in an organization. While we will share our overall findings and recommendations, individual responses will be held in strict confidentiality.

If your context demands, you might also consider some sort of code scheme that allows respondents to select others not by an alphanumeric ID. This could be a randomly generated number, or it might be a code that assists the researcher in identifying the formal position (role) of the person. Or, to protect identities, you might offer to change the names of the individuals as well as the organization in the report.

But such statements and code schemes are no substitute for the analyst, consultant, or researcher establishing their trustworthiness with respondents by spending some time with them and getting to know about them and their organization. The key is to identify their concerns and then construct the survey accordingly.

5.1.d Convenience

While each survey must be tailored to the specific group under study, the basic framework is general to all situations, and is designed to maximize the convenience to the respondents. We want to ask them to identify their social relations, in terms both of who they are tied to and of who is tied to them. We might do so by providing a checklist for them of the names of all other persons in the group, and we ask them to check off all those who meet a specific criterion. This would be especially convenient if the group is small and anonymity is not seen as important. For example, we might ask who they talk with about work-related matters every day. All right, that was a test of whether you are paying attention; you should have thought to yourself: 'That's a bad question'.

We provide our instructions like this:

> Members of organizations talk with others members about work. Below is a list of the other members of your organization. Along the left-hand side, please check those others with whom you talk about the schedule for upcoming meetings, typically every week. You should place a check next to each person you talk with about the schedule of meetings, typically every week. That is, please check all those for whom the question applies.

The above wording is a bit better: more specific and behavioral. The wording implies that such communication is an undirected social relation. This means that the relation is symmetric – both parties play the same role in the underlying activity or exchange. Undirected relations are necessarily mutual or, in other words, reciprocal.

As we've noted, other relations are directed, that is, it matters which person is initiating the contact and what role each person plays or what each brings to the exchange. Hence, we have to distinguish these roles in our questions. For example, if we want to ask about advice, it is different if Bob goes to Mari for advice than if Mari goes to Bob. If Bob goes to Mari, then Bob is in the role of needing help, while Mari is in the role of expert. These are different roles, so the exchange is asymmetric. Further, it need not be reciprocal, as Mari may never need to ask Bob for advice even though Bob needs help from Mari.

For such directional questions, we need to ask them to check off names of others they go to and of others who come to them. We do so by listing the names and putting checkboxes on both sides, along with instructions such as the following:

> Members of organizations often go to others in the organization to seek technical information needed in the course of doing their jobs. Other members often provide such information when sought. Below is a list of the other members of your organization. Along the left-hand side, please check those others to whom

you go at least once a week to get information needed to perform your job. Along the right-hand side, please identify those who come to you at least once a week seeking information they need to perform their job. You should place a check next to each person you go to, or who comes to you, at least once a week. That is, please check all those for whom the question applies. For those who both come to you and you go to, please check next to their name on both the left and the right sides.

Note that the above example wordings are especially verbose, intended to show you how detailed you may need to be if your audience is unaccustomed to dealing with a survey like this and if you are unable to provide any oral instructions to accompany the written survey. If you are able to administer the survey in person, then you may be able to streamline the written instructions considerably. Doing so would be desirable, as it would make the survey appear shorter and less burdensome – that is, more convenient.

Here's a mock-up of a network survey question using the checklist format:

> On the left-hand side, please check those to whom you go on a weekly basis when you need to know the tensile strength of a material.
> On the right-hand side, please check those who come to you on a weekly basis when they need to know which materials are in stock.

_____	Bob Jameson	_____
_____	Sarah Longhart	_____
_____	Sam Smith	_____
_____	Buddy Holly	_____
_____	Mari Hang	_____
_____	Martha Morehouse	_____

Notice the asymmetry in the wording of the goes to (left-hand) and comes to (right-hand) parts of the question. While not always the case, this is entirely possible for a directed relation. If you present questions that show you understand the context, you will increase the likelihood of getting good responses.

Let's say there are seven persons in the group you are using: Bob Jameson, Sarah Longhart, Sam Smith, Buddy Holly, Mari Hang, Martha Morehouse, and Philip Tsosi. The above format would be given to Philip, as his is the omitted name. Each person should be presented with a checklist of the other six names, with their own name omitted. Names should be presented in some sensible order, depending on the size of the group and how casually they address one another; again, context matters. Possibilities include in order of rank in the organization, perhaps grouped by departments, or alphabetically, either by first or by last name.

Within this framework, we can ask both directional and non-directional questions, such as those below:

- Undirected:
   Who do you talk with at work, typically every day, about company news and events?
   Who do you go to lunch with at least once a week?

- Directed: i. ego goes to alter; ii. alter comes to ego:
   i.   In whom do you confide your concerns about sensitive work-related issues?
   ii. Who confides in you their concerns about sensitive work-related issues?
   i.   Who have you gone to for support for a proposal that could be unpopular?
   ii. Who has come to you for support on a proposal that could be unpopular?
   i.   Who do you depend on to do their job in order for you to do yours?
   ii. Who depends on you to do your job in order to do their job well?
   i.   Who do you go to at work to find out about company news and events?
   ii. Who comes to you to find out about company news and events?

Note that these are just sample questions, of general form. In actually using them as part of a network survey for a particular group, we may want to define more specifically what we mean by 'sensitive', and so forth.

The checklist format works especially well for smaller groups when anonymity is not as important. A variation is to list the names row-wise and ask respondents to circle those for whom the question applies, known as the circle names format. If names are listed across as well as down the page, this can save a considerable amount of space.

> For each question below, please circle the names of those for whom the questions apply.
>
> Who do you go to on a weekly basis to find the tensile strength of a material?
> Bob Buddy Mari Martha Phil Sam Sarah
> Who comes to you each month to find what materials are in stock?
> Bob Buddy Mari Martha Phil Sam Sarah

For large groups, it may well be easier for respondents just to fill in blanks with names of those who fit a particular description, rather than having to scan through a long list of names. When anonymity is more important than convenience, use of an ID system along with a fill-in-the-blanks format works best. A mock-up of a fill-in-names format is shown below:

For each question below, you will be provided with nine blanks. Please fill in the blanks with the names of others in your organization for whom the question applies. If there are fewer than nine others for whom the question applies, you may leave blanks empty. If there are more than nine others for whom the question applies, please list the nine who best meet the criteria.

Please fill in the names of others in your organization who typically provide you with information about company news and events.

_____	_____	_____
_____	_____	_____
_____	_____	_____

Please fill in the names of others in your organization who you typically provide with information about company news and events.

_____	_____	_____
_____	_____	_____
_____	_____	_____

The number of blanks to leave should be determined by the size of the group and the organizational or group context. That is, before constructing the questionnaire, use interviews, observations, or pilot surveys to get a sense of how many contacts group members typically have.

5.2   Individual data: ask, observe, inspect

Social networks do not treat everyone the same for all purposes. Instead, network effects are contingent on characteristics of the actors as well as on the purposes of the social interaction. The nature of the participants and how the ties are embedded in the overall structure, for instance, determine whether cohesive ties give a broader bandwidth for support, or act as an echo chamber.

In conjunction with or as part of the survey, then, you'll want to obtain some data on the individuals, their human capital, work roles, and background characteristics. We'll discuss how we use such data in detail in the next chapters. For now, be aware that you should collect such data at the same time as the relational data, as part of the network survey. Let's give you a sense of what to ask about.

Broadly speaking, individual characteristics can be classified into two categories. Attributes include:

- demographics, such as age, race, gender, ethnicity, and so forth;
- human capital, such as education and experience;
- personality traits and attitudes.

Affiliations include:

- membership in groups or organizations, such as community groups, occupations, or schools;
- attendance at events, such as meetings, conferences, and so forth;
- interests in subjects, of any kind.

Whereas the relational questions must be obtained by asking respondents directly about their own interactions, individual data may be obtained in a number of ways. Some items may be obtained by observation, such as gender or ethnicity. Other items may be gotten from company records. In the optics firm example, we have two attributes: organizational level and division. Note that we obtained these from company records, rather than by asking the workers directly.

We may, of course, be able to get some information only by asking respondents directly. In that case, we would typically include the items as part of the survey instrument.

In the undergraduate cohort example, a variety of attributes and affiliations was obtained. Personal interests and roles were asked as part of the survey, demographics were taken from university records, and affiliations were taken from the membership lists of key organizations.

Having obtained both relational and individual data, it still has to be prepared for processing. We do this in the next chapter.

6 Handling data I: preparations

Having obtained both individual and relational data, the next step is to prepare it for analysis. This involves entering, cross-checking, and possibly transforming the responses. We'll cover the relational responses first, both in preparing them for computer entry and in the initial processing. We'll then turn to how to enter and transform individual characteristics to turn them into relational data.

I PREPARING RELATIONAL DATA

6.1 Entering and cross-checking responses

Once you have your network survey written, according to the four principles of construction (content, context, confidentiality, and convenience), the next step is to administer the survey. To administer the survey, we simply mean to hand it out and collect the responses. But even this might not be quite that simple, as you may have to take some time to explain it to members of the group and you may need to remind some members that it's important; it may take some gentle prompting to make sure they get it done in a timely fashion.

Once the responses are in hand, you'll need to prepare the data so that it can be processed by the computer. This means entering the responses as given and then cross-checking them. For example, if Bob says he goes to Mari for advice, we check to see whether Mari also reports that Bob comes to her. If so, then the relation is most likely correct. If there is any discrepancy (say Mari does not report that Bob comes to her, even though Bob says he does), then, according to our general rule, it is likely that the relation doesn't exist and we should treat it as such unless we have other evidence that Bob is a more credible respondent than Mari.

Director survey
Let's look at data from a relational survey of the board of directors for a bank, consisting of seven members, Bob Jameson, Sarah Longhart, Sam Smith, Buddy Holly, Mari Hang, Martha Morehouse, and Philip Tsosi. Imagine you asked them to check along the left-hand side all of the other members of their group for whom this communication question applies: 'Who do you talk with about upcoming events at work, typically three days or more each week?' Figure 6.1 shows the surveys they return to you.

Now you'll need to get ready to handle the relational data.

Bob's:	Buddy's:	Mari's:
Buddy	Bob	Bob
Mari	Mari	Buddy
Martha	Martha	Martha
Philip	✓Philip	✓Philip
✓Sam	Sam	✓Sam
Sarah	✓Sarah	✓Sarah

Martha's:	Philip's:	Sam's:	Sarah's:
Bob	Bob	✓Bob	Bob
Buddy	✓Buddy	Buddy	✓Buddy
Mari	✓Mari	✓Mari	✓Mari
✓Philip	✓Martha	Martha	Martha
Sam	Sam	Philip	Philip
✓Sarah	Sarah	✓Sarah	✓Sam

Figure 6.1   Director communication survey responses

Input the responses

For each question, we input the responses into a spreadsheet where individuals anchor both the rows and the columns. So, for our board of directors, consisting of Bob, Buddy, Mari, Martha, Philip, Sam, and Sarah, we would have a 7 × 7 spreadsheet, with one row and one column for each of the members of the group. You would also add one initial row and one initial column for the names of your group members. List the individuals in the same order across columns and down rows. We call such a spreadsheet an adjacency matrix.

You'll have a separate spreadsheet, or adjacency matrix, for each type of network: communication, trust, and advice. For each, we want the cell entries to indicate the presence or absence of a social relation of the particular type between the persons anchoring the row and column for each cell. The result will be a matrix of 0s and 1s, with 0 indicating the absence of the relation and 1 indicating the presence of the relation.

Such an adjacency matrix, consisting of just the two values 0 and 1, is called a binary adjacency matrix. In this text, we will primarily be concerned with constructing and analyzing binary adjacency matrices. In general, an adjacency matrix could also be valued. In a valued adjacency matrix, the cell entries can be any non-negative integer, indicating the strength or number of relations of a particular type or types.

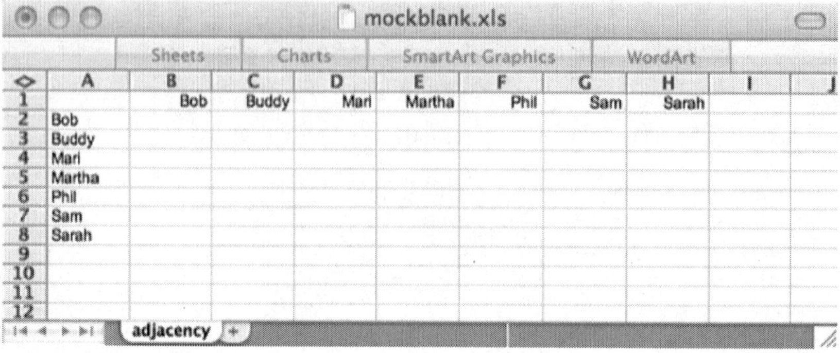

Figure 6.2   Blank adjacency matrix

For our purposes, we also need to distinguish between directed and undirected relations, which in turn produce directed and undirected adjacency matrices, respectively. *Directed* adjacency matrices are those for which the relation can exist from person A to person B without it necessarily also existing in the same way from person B to person A (we typically think of advice as directed, for example). An *undirected* adjacency matrix is one for which the social relation cannot exist unless it is mutual for both parties (communication is often thought of as undirected).

6.2   Undirected relations

Let's say we are filling in the communication network spreadsheet for our director survey responses and assume for the moment that the relation occurs and hence the question is worded in an undirected way (e.g. 'Who do you talk with about . . . ?'). So constructed, the diagonal elements would correspond to whether a person talks with him- or herself, and so just enter all 0s. Off-diagonal elements correspond to whether the row person talks with the column person. Enter the data from each person's survey across the row for that person, entering 0 if they do not report talking with the column person, and entering 1 if they do report talking with them.

Let's walk through a couple of respondents' surveys to see how the above matrix came together. In the survey responses, look for Bob's survey and refer to Figures 6.3 and 6.4. You can see that Bob has placed a check only in front of Sam. Now look at Figure 6.4. You can see that in Bob's row there is a 1 only in the column labeled Sam.

In Buddy's survey responses (Figure 6.1), he has placed checks in front of Philip and Sarah. Looking at the adjacency matrix in Figure 6.5, we find that, in Buddy's row, there are 1s only in the columns labeled Philip and

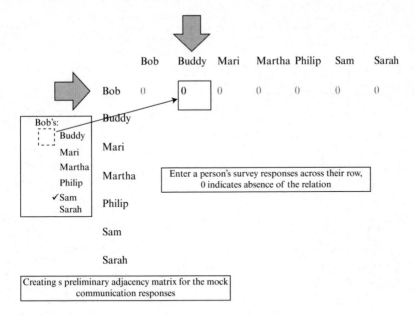

Figure 6.3   Entering absence of an undirected relationship

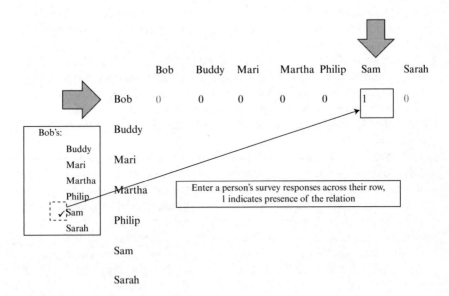

Figure 6.4   Entering presence of an undirected relationship

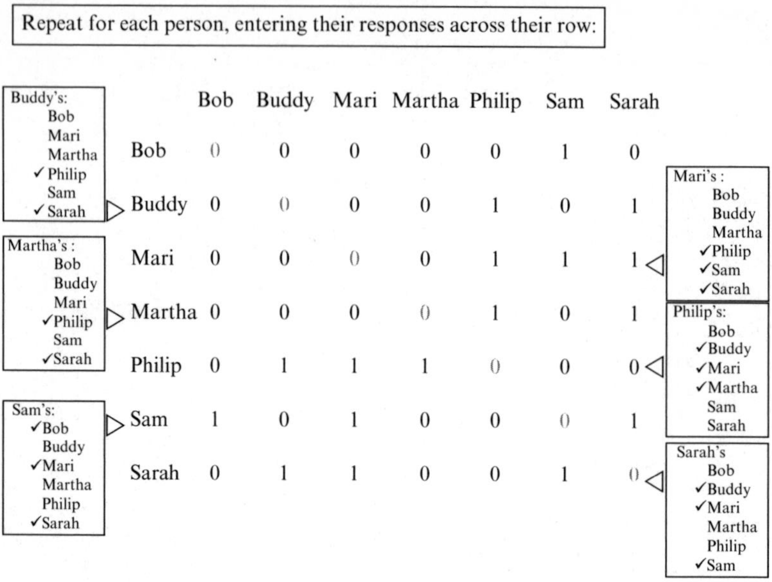

Repeat for each person, entering their responses across their row:

Buddy's:
Bob
Mari
Martha
✓Philip
Sam
✓Sarah

Martha's:
Bob
Buddy
Mari
✓Philip
Sam
✓Sarah

Sam's:
✓Bob
Buddy
✓Mari
Martha
Philip
✓Sarah

	Bob	Buddy	Mari	Martha	Philip	Sam	Sarah
Bob	0	0	0	0	0	1	0
Buddy	0	0	0	0	1	0	1
Mari	0	0	0	0	1	1	1
Martha	0	0	0	0	1	0	1
Philip	0	1	1	1	0	0	0
Sam	1	0	1	0	0	0	1
Sarah	0	1	1	0	0	1	0

Mari's:
Bob
Buddy
Martha
✓Philip
✓Sam
✓Sarah

Philip's:
Bob
✓Buddy
✓Mari
✓Martha
Sam
Sarah

Sarah's
Bob
✓Buddy
✓Mari
Martha
Philip
✓Sam

Figure 6.5   Filling in an undirected adjacency matrix

Sarah. Continuing with the others' responses, you should find 1s in the respondent's row where he or she has placed a check in front of the name that goes with the column label.

Entering all the group members' survey responses across the rows gives us a preliminary adjacency matrix for the activity they were questioned about (refer to Figure 6.5). We then enter all 0s along the diagonal as in Figure 6.6, since relations a person has with his or her own self are not social ties. Having done so, we have the preliminary adjacency matrix in Figure 6.7.

The matrix in Figure 6.7 is preliminary in that we need to cross-check the responses for consistency between responders. In other words, both parties to a relation need to report the relation as the same. When a question is undirected, we can cross-check responses simply by checking to see if the matrix is symmetric. That is, if there is a 1 in column j for row i, then there must also be a 1 in column i of row j. For instance, if Bob says he talks with Sam, then Sam must say he talks with Bob. Formalized, the requirement for symmetric matrices is that cell(i,j)=cell(j,i) for all i,j. In words, the matrix must equal its transpose (Figure 6.8).

If cells (i,j) and (j,i) do not correspond, then the general rule is to set them both to 0. This is because research and practical experience have demonstrated that there is more of a bias to over-respond than to

And enter all 0's for the diagonal:

	Bob	Buddy	Mari	Martha	Philip	Sam	Sarah
Bob	0	0	0	0	0	1	0
Buddy	0	0	0	0	1	0	1
Mari	0	0	0	0	1	1	1
Martha	0	0	0	0	1	0	1
Philip	0	1	1	1	0	0	0
Sam	1	0	1	0	0	0	1
Sarah	0	1	1	0	0	1	0

Figure 6.6   Diagonal entries are set to 0

Creates a preliminary adjacency matrix for communication

	Bob	Buddy	Mari	Martha	Philip	Sam	Sarah
Bob	0	0	0	0	0	1	0
Buddy	0	0	0	0	1	0	1
Mari	0	0	0	0	1	1	1
Martha	0	0	0	0	1	0	1
Philip	0	1	1	1	0	0	0
Sam	1	0	1	0	0	0	1
Sarah	0	1	1	0	0	1	0

Figure 6.7   Preliminary undirected adjacency matrix

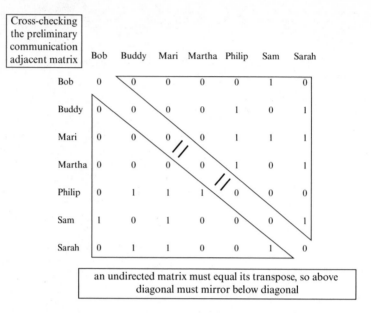

Cross-checking the preliminary communication adjacent matrix	Bob	Buddy	Mari	Martha	Philip	Sam	Sarah
Bob	0	0	0	0	0	1	0
Buddy	0	0	0	0	1	0	1
Mari	0	0	0	0	1	1	1
Martha	0	0	0	0	1	0	1
Philip	0	1	1	1	0	0	0
Sam	1	0	1	0	0	0	1
Sarah	0	1	1	0	0	1	0

an undirected matrix must equal its transpose, so above diagonal must mirror below diagonal

Figure 6.8   Preparing to cross-check an undirected matrix

under-respond. A tendency to want to look popular and a tendency to want to appear inclusive (not leave someone out) are two sources of over-response bias. However, if you know about the individuals and feel that one of the respondents is more accurate, then you can set the cell entries according to the more credible respondent's answer.

Cross-checking the preliminary communication adjacency matrix, we look to see if the matrix is symmetric around the diagonal. That is, we should be able to place a mirror on the diagonal and see the same entires as we originally placed. Figure 6.9 provides an illustration. Equivalently, we can overlay the original and transposed versions of the preliminary undirected adjacency matrix.

Referring to Figure 6.9 and Figure 6.10, looking across the row for Bob, we see that Bob says he talks to Sam; Sam also reports he talks with Bob (looking down the column labeled Bob). Looking across the row for Buddy, we see that Buddy says he talks with Philip and Sarah; Philip and Sarah each say they talk with Buddy (looking down the column labeled Buddy). Continuing in this way, all relations cross-check except for that between Martha and Sarah. Looking across the row for Martha, we see she reports talking to Philip and Sarah; but, looking down the column labeled Martha, we find only Philip reports talking to Martha, and Sarah does not. That is, cell (4,7)=1, but cell (7,4)=0. So the matrix is not symmetrical

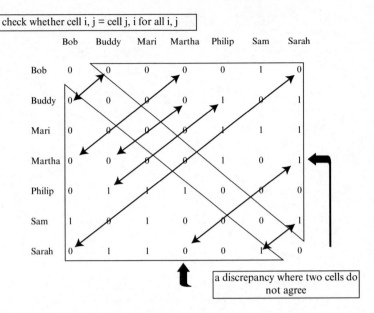

Figure 6.9   Cross-checking an undirected matrix

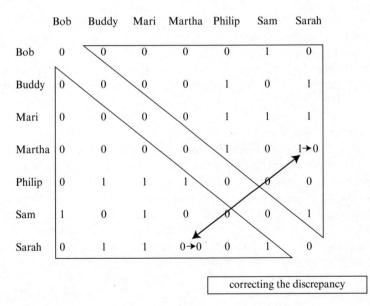

Figure 6.10   Adjusting a discrepancy in an undirected adjacency matrix

	Bob	Buddy	Mari	Martha	Philip	Sam	Sarah
The final undirected communication adjacency matrix							
Bob	0	0	0	0	0	1	0
Buddy	0	0	0	0	1	0	1
Mari	0	0	0	0	1	1	1
Martha	0	0	0	0	1	0	1
Philip	0	1	1	1	0	0	0
Sam	1	0	1	0	0	0	1
Sarah	0	1	1	0	0	1	0

Figure 6.11   Final undirected adjacency matrix for director communication

around the diagonal. Unless we have other information, we correct this by setting cell (4,7) to 0 (Figure 6.10).

You should also double-check that the diagonal entries are all 0. That is, cell(i,i)=0 for all i. That done, your final adjacency matrix for communication would look like Figure 6.11.

6.3   Directed relations

We now consider how to handle responses for a directed relation, using our board of directors. Imagine now that you ask them an advice question, to check along the left-hand side all of the other members of their group whom they '. . . go to almost every week for technical information, such as capital reserve requirements, needed to do your job'. Along the right-hand side, you ask them to check off all the members for whom this question applies: 'Who comes to you when they need information on capital requirements or availability in doing their job more than once a week?' Figure 6.12 presents the surveys they return to you.

Entering and cross-checking adjacency matrices for directional questions is more complicated, because by definition such relations need not be symmetric or reciprocal. For directed questions (such as the advice question), across a row you would enter whether the row person reports going

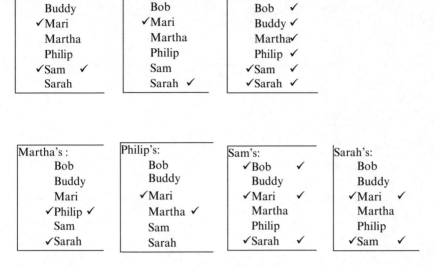

Figure 6.12   Director advice survey responses

to the column person for that relation. That is, as set up in the director survey responses, you would enter the left-hand responses across the row. Doing so results in the preliminary 'goes to' adjacency matrix for advice shown in Figure 6.13.

Notice how we got this again. For the advice survey responses, look at Bob's. Bob has placed checks along the left-hand side of Mari's and Sam's names, so we put 1s in Bob's row under the columns labeled for Mari and Sam. We follow the same process for each person's responses.

Again, we should double-check that the diagonal entries are all 0, as otherwise we have gotten mixed up somewhere. We should also cross-check the responses, but we do so differently for directed relations, since the adjacency matrix does not need to be symmetric. Instead, we do so by also entering down each column whether the column person reports that the row person comes to them. That is, you would enter the right-hand responses from the returned surveys down the column labeled for the person who responded on each form, as illustrated in Figures 6.14 and 6.15. Doing so using the attached survey responses results in the cross-check 'comes to' adjacency matrix for advice shown in Figure 6.16.

Looking at Bob's set of responses on the advice surveys, we see he placed a check only along the right-hand side of Sam. So we go down Bob's column and place a 1 in the row labeled Sam. As we do so, we check

Entering each person's left-hand (goes to) responses across their row results in the preliminary, directed, 'goes to' adjacency matrix for the mock advice surveys:

Buddy's:
Bob
✓Mari
Martha
Philip
Sam
Sarah ✓

Martha's:
Bob
Buddy
Mari
✓Philip ✓
Sam
✓Sarah

Sam's:
✓Bob ✓
Buddy
✓Mari ✓
Martha
Philip
✓Sarah ✓

Mari's:
Bob ✓
Buddy ✓
Martha✓
Philip ✓
✓Sam ✓
✓Sarah ✓

Philip's:
Bob
Buddy
✓Mari
Martha ✓
Sam
Sarah

Sarah's:
Bob
Buddy
✓Mari ✓
Martha
Philip
✓Sam ✓

	Bob	Buddy	Mari	Martha	Philip	Sam	Sarah
Bob	0	0	1	0	0	1	0
▷ Buddy	0	0	1	0	0	0	0
Mari	0	0	0	0	0	1	1 ◁
▷ Martha	0	0	0	0	1	0	1
Philip	0	0	1	0	0	0	0 ◁
▷ Sam	1	0	1	0	0	0	1
Sarah	0	0	1	0	0	1	0 ◁

Figure 6.13   Preliminary directed 'goes to' adjacency matrix for director advice

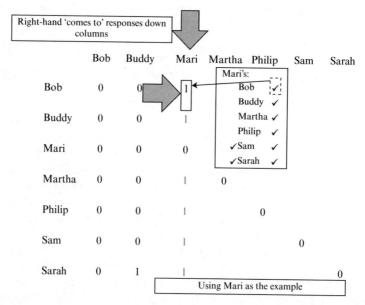

Figure 6.14   Entering 'comes to' responses down a column

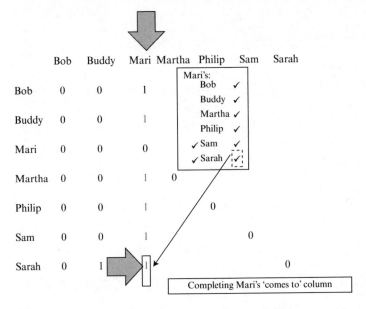

Figure 6.15   Entering right-hand responses down a column

Repeat to get this preliminary 'comes to' matrix.

	Bob	Buddy	Mari	Martha	Philip	Sam	Sarah
Bob	0	0	1	0	0	1	0
Buddy	0	0	1	0	0	0	0
Mari	0	0	0	0	0	1	1
Martha	0	0	1	0	1	0	0
Philip	0	0	1	1	0	0	0
Sam	1	0	1	0	0	0	1
Sarah	0	1	1	0	0	1	0

Figure 6.16   A preliminary directed 'comes to' adjacency matrix

	Bob	Buddy	Mari	Martha	Philip	Sam	Sarah
Bob	0 0	0 0	1 1	0 0	0 0	1 1	0 0
Buddy	0 0	0 0	1 1	0 0	0 0	0 0	0 0
Mari	0 0	0 0	0 0	0 0	0 0	1 1	1 1
Martha	0 0	0 0	0 1	0 0	1 1	0 0	1 0
Philip	0 0	0 0	1 1	0 1	0 0	0 0	0 0
Sam	1 1	0 0	1 1	0 0	0 0	0 0	1 1
Sarah	0 0	0 1	1 1	0 0	0 0	1 1	0 0

For a directed relation, the 'goes to' matrix must equal the 'come to' matrix

Overlaying 'goes to' (left-hand) and 'comes to' (right-hand) reveals discrepancies

Figure 6.17   Cross-checking responses in a directed relation

to see that the cell entries (i,j) are equal when entered across the row for the left-hand entries of person i as compared to when entered down the column as right-hand responses for person j. So, if row person i reports going to the column person j for advice, there will be a 1 in cell (i,j) when we enter person i's left-hand responses. You should double-check, using the column person j's survey, whether they report, in their right-hand responses, that row person i comes to them, which should also lead to a 1 in cell (i,j).

We can facilitate this comparison by overlaying the 'comes to' responses on to the preliminary matrix we formed using the 'goes to' responses, as in Figure 6.17. We can now readily see four discrepancies. In three cases, the row person did not report going to the column label, but the column person says that the row label comes to them. In one case, the row person reports going to the column label, but the column person did not report that the row label in fact comes to them. We adjust according to our general rule in Figure 6.18.

Let's review. For our advice network, we have found four inconsistencies in reporting relations:

- Sarah did not say she goes to Buddy for advice, yet Buddy says she does.

	Bob	Buddy	Mari	Martha	Philip	Sam	Sarah
Bob	0	0	1	0	0	1	0
Buddy	0	0	1	0	0	0	0
Mari	0	0	0	0	0	1	1
Martha	0	0	0/1 ➤ 0	0	1	0	1/0 ➤ 0
Philip	0	0	1	0/1 ➤ 0	0	0	0
Sam	1	0	1	0	0	0	1
Sarah	0	0/1 ➤ 0	1	0	0	1	0

> Discrepancies are corrected

Figure 6.18   Adjusting discrepancies in a directed adjacency matrix

- Martha did not say she goes to Mari for advice, yet Mari says she does.
- Philip did not say he goes to Martha for advice, yet Martha says he does.
- Martha says she goes to Sarah for advice, yet Sarah says she doesn't.

If there is a discrepancy between the left-hand entry of person i and the right-hand entry of person j over what to put in cell (i,j), then the general rule is to set them both to 0. However, you may choose to do otherwise if you feel that one of the respondents' answers is more credible. Following the general rule leads to a final adjacency matrix for advice that looks like Figure 6.19.

6.4   Combining multiple questions

What if you have more than one question for a type of network? For example, suppose you are unsure how best to capture trust, so you ask two questions about trust-related behaviors (such as i. 'Who do you typically go to for support on a proposal that might be unpopular?' and ii. 'Who do you typically share confidential information with at work?'). You want to use these two questions in combination to form a single trust network.

Resulting in the corrected adjacency matrix for advice:

	Bob	Buddy	Mari	Martha	Philip	Sam	Sarah
Bob	0	0	1	0	0	1	0
Buddy	0	0	1	0	0	0	0
Mari	0	0	0	0	0	1	1
Martha	0	0	0	0	1	0	0
Philip	0	0	1	0	0	0	0
Sam	1	0	1	0	0	0	1
Sarah	0	0	1	0	0	1	0

Figure 6.19 Final directed adjacency matrix for director advice

Two questions can be combined to form a single binary adjacency matrix either by taking the union or by taking the intersection:

- The union rule specifies that a relation exists between any pair of persons if the relation exists for either of the questions. We typically use this rule when the relation is multifaceted, that is, when more than one behavior reflects the underlying type of tie.
- The intersection rule is stricter and says that a relation exists only if the relation exists for both questions. We typically use this rule when the relation is ambiguous, that is, when we are unsure what behavior actually reflects the underlying type of tie.

Whether you use the union rule or you use the intersection rule depends on the context of your group. If neither the intersection nor the union rule seems to fit your purposes, you might also take one of these approaches:

- Examine the responses and see which question is more informative – neither too sparse nor too dense, either of which suggests a misunderstood question.
- Use all of the questions, treating them as separate, though perhaps closely related, networks.

Note, of course, that we might use other rules if we were interested in forming valued adjacency matrices. For instance, we might add together all the related matrices to form a single valued adjacency matrix in which cell entries give the number of related relations that exist between the row and column persons.

For the purpose of this class, we wish to form a single binary adjacency matrix for each of our three key types of relations (communication, advice, trust).

6.5   Saving the responses for analysis.

As noted, you can enter the data from your surveys into any spreadsheet editor (UCINET has one, but Excel will do). To do so, you should create a separate sheet with the case-by-case adjacency matrix for each type of network. For each sheet, the spreadsheet should have the group members' names across the first row and down the first column, and should contain the 0/1 cell entries beginning in the second row and column. Some dos and don'ts include:

- Do put a simple name for the relation in the upper leftmost cell of your spreadsheet (A1).
- Don't leave any empty rows or columns in or around your adjacency matrix.
- Don't use any shading or borders.
- Do name the sheet with the type of relation (e.g. Trust).
- Do the dos and don't do the don'ts for each of your networks.

6.6   Data and more data

Let's look at the optics data. We'll step in at the point where the survey has been conducted and the data initially entered, so we have a set of preliminary adjacency matrices. We want to double- and cross-check these matrices, meaning two things:

1. Double-check the data entry. We need to ensure the diagonal is all zeros.
2. Cross-check the responses. We need to ensure that an undirected adjacency matrix is symmetric around the diagonal.

A couple of tools to look for in the software package of your choice which can help in data checking are typically called diagonal and symmetrize command. Here's how to use them to cross-check responses and double-check data entry.

First, let's double-check data entry, using the diagonal command.

Recall that we expect all the diagonal values to be exactly zero, since we are not studying intraperson relations. We can extract the diagonal values both for inspection and to automatically set them to zero. Be careful not just to set them to zero without inspecting them first, as the real point is not just to ensure that they are zero but to help in locating any place that data entry might have gotten off track. If there are nonzero diagonal entries, we need to look at the other data in the vicinity (row and column) to make sure every response is in its proper row and/or column.

So set the diagonal value to be zero and note that you will need the resulting output dataset only if there are nonzero values in the diagonal. But, again, you'll also need to take a careful look at the rest of the adjacency matrix to be sure the rows or columns are not off.

Once the diagonals are double-checked and there is no evidence of mis-entered data, we can cross-check for symmetry. Be on alert that this is done only if the adjacency matrix is undirected. Now, you'll typically be able to specify a symmetrizing method. The choice here depends on how you want to treat any discrepancies. Our general rule is to set cells to zero unless both parties agree that the relation exists. Put differently, if there is a zero in either cell (i,j) or cell (j,i) then we set both to zero. Look at the choices in the drop-down menu for the method. To accomplish our general rule, we could use either the minimum or the product method.

Now, the output dataset will be a corrected adjacency matrix. As long as you want to apply the same rule to all discrepancies, you can proceed to analyze the output dataset as your network. If, however, you want to inspect individual discrepancies, you'll need to review the discrepancies first and make adjustments using the spreadsheet editor.

To find and review the discrepancies, note that discrepancies show up in the summed matrix as 1s. If there is no discrepancy, then the initial and symmetrized matrices must agree. If so, they are either both 0, giving a sum of 0, or both 1, giving a sum of 2. A sum of 1 indicates that the initial matrix was 1 and the symmetrized matrix corrected it to 0, if the general rule was applied.

We don't want to relive the cumbersome task of entering the hundreds of responses from the example study of UG cohorts, but we can use the entered data to learn some tricks for handling adjacency matrices on the computer. Let's take a look at the adjacency matrix, just to get an appreciation for the scholars who wrote the computer programs that do the work for us. That is, the programs will do the work once we've entered the data. There is no short-cut for careful data entry and cross-checking. But we'll spare you that for this example.

With large-scale networks like this, even simple tasks like checking the diagonal can be tiresome, so we can really take advantage of the computer tools. Let's assume that the matrix is otherwise correctly double- and cross-checked and ready to go. Before we proceed to any analyses, let's use our software to learn whether this is a directed or undirected relation.

Recall that an undirected relation will be symmetrical, while a directed relation need not. It follows that we can use a symmetrize tool to discover the nature of this adjacency matrix as long as we are sure that it has already been cross-checked properly. Although we'll need to produce a symmetrized matrix along the way, we'll want to use only the initial matrix for analysis. In this case, the relation was already cross-checked, and so symmetrizing it for analysis would be inappropriate. The purpose of using the tool is diagnostic only.

To answer the question of whether this is a directed relation, we can use the percentage of symmetric pairs reported by, for example, UCINET or Pajek. Anything less than 100 percent indicates a diagnosis that the matrix is not symmetric. Talking most frequently to others is a social relation that must occur in a directed way for this population.

II PREPARING INDIVIDUAL DATA

To examine the social processes of *formative bases*, we need to transform the individual level data to dyadic measures of similarity or dissimilarity that can be correlated to, or regressed on, social relations. For our purposes, recall that individual characteristics can be classified into two broad types: attributes and affiliations. The rules for transforming individual level data to dyadic measures vary by whether the data are attributes or affiliations.

6.7   Attributes
Attribute variables can be numerical or categorical, and can be single item measures (such as age or gender) or may consist of multiple items for a single attribute (such as personality or attitudes).

Single item attribute measures can be entered into a combined spreadsheet, in the standard format where rows are persons and columns are variables. To convert single item, individual attribute data to dyadic similarity or dissimilarity data, we use these rules:

1. match for categorical as a measure of similarity;
2. absolute difference for numerical as a measure of dissimilarity.

The match rule converts individual data to dyadic by placing a 1 in cell (i,j) if person i and person j match in terms of the category that describes each on the measure. For example, if the individual attribute is gender, then if both parties to a dyad are the same gender they are a match and we set their dyad similarity to 1; if the two persons are of opposite sex, then they do not match and we set the dyad similarity to 0.

The absolute difference rule converts individual data to the dyad level by taking the absolute value of the difference between person i and person j in cell (i,j). For example, if one person is 20 years old and the second is 25 years old, then the absolute difference of 5 years tells us how dissimilar they are to one another on the attribute.

For multiple item attributes, each attribute needs to be given a separate spreadsheet, with rows as persons and columns as the multiple measures for that attribute.

To convert multi-item individual attributes to dyad level relational measures of similarity of dissimilarity, we use these rules:

1. match for small set of categorical variables;
2. Euclidean distance for small set of numerical variables, or small to large set of categorical variables;
3. correlation for large set of numerical variables.

The match rule sets cell (i,j) to 1 only if person i and person j match in terms of their category on all items, producing a single similarity measure for the multi-item attribute.

The Euclidean distance rule produces a dissimilarity measure for dyad (i,j) by taking the squared difference between person i and person j for their responses to each item, summing these squared differences, and then taking the square root of the sum of squared differences.

The correlation rule produces a similarity measure for dyad (i,j) by correlating person i's vector of responses with person j's vector of responses.

Let's take a look at some attribute data for our fictive group of seven: Bob, Buddy, Mari, Martha, Phil, Sam, and Sarah. Imagine they had the data shown in Table 6.1 on age (years), gender (0=male, 1=female), education (1=HS, 2=UG, 3=MA), experience (years), position (1=TRAINEE, 2=LINE, 3=STAFF, 4=SUPV), and aptitude (a three item construct, with each item rated on a 1–5 scale).

To handle this data, we need to put the single item measures (age, gender, education, experience, and position) into a spreadsheet. The multi-item attribute (aptitude) needs to be put into its own separate spreadsheet. We then import each into a computer software package for network analysis, such as UCINET or Pajek.

Let's take a look at age, a single item numerical attribute. Converting to a dyadic dissimilarity using the absolute difference rule leads to the dissimilarity matrix in Table 6.2.

Table 6.1   Attribute data

	Age	Gender	Education	Experience	Position	Aptitude		
						A1	A2	A3
Bob	25	0	1	1	1	4	4	4
Buddy	36	0	2	7	2	3	4	4
Mari	35	1	3	5	3	5	5	5
Martha	45	1	1	15	2	3	3	3
Phil	42	0	2	10	4	4	4	5
Sam	33	0	2	2	2	5	3	4
Sarah	30	1	2	5	2	4	3	4

Table 6.2   Age dissimilarity matrix

	Bob	Buddy	Mari	Martha	Phil	Sam	Sarah
Bob	0	11	10	20	17	8	5
Buddy	11	0	1	9	6	3	6
Mari	10	1	0	10	7	2	5
Martha	20	9	10	0	3	12	15
Phil	17	6	7	3	0	9	12
Sam	8	3	2	12	9	0	3
Sarah	5	6	5	15	12	3	0

Network software packages will do the work for us. Look for a command to convert attribute data to a dyadic matrix. See Hanneman and Riddle (2005) or Batagelj and Mrvar (2009). Doing so, you should be able to get the matrix shown in Table 6.3.

Let's convert the single item categorical variable gender to a dyadic similarity matrix. Doing so produces the similarity matrix in Table 6.4.

Note that these similarity/dissimilarity matrices have the same structure as our adjacency matrices: they have the same number and order of rows and columns. Because of this, we can regress our adjacency matrices on such similarity/dissimilarity matrices to test for homophily/heterophily in the relations that define adjacency in the network matrices.

Education is an ordinal variable, so we could treat it either as categorical, using the match rule to produce dyadic similarities, or as numerical, using absolute differences to produce dyadic dissimilarities. Experience is clearly numerical; position is clearly categorical (although there might be an order between trainee, line, and supervisory; staff does not fit in order, so the variable can be treated only as categorical). We would create our

Table 6.3   Gender similarity matrix

	Bob	Buddy	Mari	Martha	Phil	Sam	Sarah
Bob	1	1	0	0	1	1	0
Buddy	1	1	0	0	1	1	0
Mari	0	0	1	1	0	0	1
Martha	0	0	1	1	0	0	1
Phil	1	1	0	0	1	1	0
Sam	1	1	0	0	1	1	0
Sarah	0	0	1	1	0	0	1

Table 6.4   Aptitude dissimilarity matrix

	Bob	Buddy	Mari	Martha	Phil	Sam	Sarah
Bob	0	1	1.73	1.73	1	1.41	1
Buddy	1	0	2.45	1.41	1.41	2.24	1.41
Mari	1.73	2.45	0	3.46	1.41	2.24	2.45
Martha	1.73	1.41	3.46	0	2.45	2.24	1.41
Phil	1	1.41	1.41	2.45	0	1.73	1.41
Sam	1.41	2.24	2.24	2.24	1.73	0	1
Sarah	1	1.41	2.45	1.41	1.41	1	0

dyadic similarity/dissimilarity matrices in the same manner as for age and gender.

Aptitude is a multi-item measure, consisting of three factors (perhaps verbal, math, and analytical) and so is treated according to the rules for multi-item attributes. For a small set of numerical variables, we form a dissimilarity matrix using Euclidean distance. We'll save these matrices to test for age, gender, and aptitude homophily/heterophily, as well as exploring individual differences in social capital.

The only attributes we have for the optics data are the formal positions, in terms of level and division. Each employee belongs to one of four divisions (coded 1–4 from left to right across the organization chart in Chapter 1) and is either an executive (SVP=2 or President=3) or not (=1). Given that level is an ordinal variable, we can use the absolute difference or we could try using exact matches. For division, since this is a categorical variable, we will opt for the match rule. Table 6.5 shows a similarity matrix based on division. A quick look should show that employees in the same division have a 1 for their dyad, and those not in the same division should have 0.

Next, let's look at how we handle affiliation data.

Table 6.5   Optics firm division match matrix

	Barton	Mullaney	Petersen	Levy	Conn	Bahr	Rodrigues	Oaxaca	Cottrel	Lehman	Angus
Barton	1	0	0	0	0	0	0	0	0	0	0
Mullaney (SVP)	0	1	0	0	0	1	1	1	0	0	0
Petersen (SVP)	0	0	1	0	0	0	0	0	1	1	1
Levy (SVP)	0	0	0	1	0	0	0	0	0	0	0
Conn (SVP)	0	0	0	0	1	0	0	0	0	0	0
Bahr	0	1	0	0	0	1	1	1	0	0	0
Rodrigues	0	1	0	0	0	1	1	1	0	0	0
Oaxaca	0	1	0	0	0	1	1	1	0	0	0
Cottrel	0	0	1	0	0	0	0	0	1	1	1
Lehman	0	0	1	0	0	0	0	0	1	1	1
Angus	0	0	1	0	0	0	0	0	1	1	1

Table 6.6   Affiliation data

	O1	O2	O3	O4	O5
Bob	0	0	0	0	0
Buddy	1	1	0	0	0
Mari	0	0	1	1	0
Martha	1	1	0	0	1
Phil	1	0	1	0	1
Sam	0	0	1	0	0
Sarah	0	0	1	1	1

6.8   Affiliations

Affiliational data are always dichotomous, coded 0/1 for absence/presence of membership, attendance, or interest. These data can then be:

- taken together, as a multi-item measure of common affiliation; or
- taken separately for single affiliations of particular interest; or
- grouped into sets of affiliations that go together.

Affiliational variables that are to be taken together to form a single co-affiliation measure can be entered in a combined spreadsheet. Affiliational variables of special interest should be given their own spreadsheet (or single item affiliations can be handled as attributes and entered in the spreadsheet with other single item attributes).

To convert individual affiliations to a dyadic measure, we transpose and multiply the individual actor by variable incidence matrix which, through the wonders of matrix algebra, results in a dyadic similarity matrix giving the number of common affiliations for dyad (i,j).

Let's say there are five community organizations that our group members belong to, as shown in Table 6.6.

To have a computer package perform the matrix manipulations needed to get our dyadic co-membership similarity matrix, look for a command to convert affiliation data. Doing so, you'll get the dyadic similarity matrix in Table 6.7.

Using the rules we've covered, any kind of individual characteristics can be transformed into dyadic measures of similarity or dissimilarity. Social relations are dyadic by their very nature. To analyze the role that individual characteristics play in social capital, thus, requires us to prepare the data in this way.

We'll end this chapter with the board of directors' responses to a question about their trust relations. They were asked to check who they go to

Table 6.7 Common affiliation matrix

	Bob	Buddy	Mari	Martha	Phil	Sam	Sarah
Bob	0	0	0	0	0	0	0
Buddy	0	2	0	2	1	0	0
Mari	0	0	2	0	1	1	2
Martha	0	2	0	3	2	0	1
Phil	0	1	1	2	3	1	2
Sam	0	0	1	0	1	1	1
Sarah	0	0	2	1	2	1	3

Bob's:
- ✓Buddy
- Mari
- Martha
- Philip
- Sam ✓
- ✓Sarah

Buddy's:
- Bob ✓
- Mari
- Martha
- ✓Philip ✓
- Sam
- ✓Sarah ✓

Mari's :
- Bob
- Buddy
- Martha
- Philip
- ✓Sam
- Sarah ✓

Martha's :
- Bob
- Buddy
- Mari
- ✓Philip✓
- Sam
- Sarah

Philip's:
- Bob
- ✓Buddy ✓
- Mari
- Martha ✓
- Sam
- Sarah

Sam's:
- ✓Bob ✓
- Buddy
- Mari
- Martha
- Philip
- ✓Sarah ✓

Sarah's:
- Bob ✓
- ✓Buddy ✓
- ✓Mari
- Martha
- Philip
- ✓Sam ✓

Figure 6.20 Director trust survey responses

when they first have concerns about inadequate capital reserves, and who comes to them with such concerns. The returned surveys are presented in Figure 6.20. You should be prepared to prepare this data before moving on to the next chapter.

7 Handling data II: visualizations

We are almost ready to begin analyzing network data. The first step in processing the data will be to get the network visualization, or map. In order to both draw and read such a map, we need some more terminology.

7.1 Terminology

A *graph* is a visual representation of the members of a group and the relations between them. When dealing with social relations, this is referred to as a *sociograph* or, in early work, sociogram.

A graph represents each person as a *point*, also called a node or vertex. Each relation that exists, or tie, is represented as a *line* (also called a link or edge). Lines can correspond to any type of social relation. Lines can be undirected or directed, binary or valued.

An undirected line exists when the tie has no direction, that is, the relationship is mutual and reciprocal. Directed lines occur when one party has a relation to a second, but the second need not have the same relation to the first. A directed line might occur, for instance, if a trainee asks a mentor for help. The existence of the trainee's tie to the mentor does not require, or expect, the mentor to ask the trainee for help in the same way. The mentor has an advice-giving tie to the trainee, which is different than the advice-seeking tie the trainee has to the mentor.

Binary lines simply indicate the existence of a relationship, whereas valued lines indicate the strength, volume, intensity, or frequency, for example. Another example of a valued line would occur when we aggregate so that the relationship being graphed is the sum over all types of whether you have each type of relationship. Then the value of a line would be the multiplicity, or number, of relations involved. When a graph can have directional lines, it is sometimes referred to as a digraph. Similarly, when a graph can have valued lines, it is referred to as a valued graph.

Two points, or persons, that are connected by a line, or relation, are said to be *adjacent* to one another. Those points to which a particular point is adjacent are termed its *neighborhood*.

Points may be directly connected by a line, or they may be indirectly connected through a sequence of lines. A sequence of lines is a *walk*, and a walk in which each point and each line are distinct is called a *path*. The number of lines that make up a path is referred to as its *length*. The shortest path between any two points is referred to as a *geodesic*. The length of the geodesic between two points is the *distance* between them.

7.2   Getting a graph

Let's start by getting sociographs for our group consisting of Bob, Buddy, Mari, Martha, Phil, Sam, and Sarah.

There are a number of algorithms available in computer programs, such as the one we'll be using (NetDraw), but it is worth talking a bit about the principles that underlie these algorithms (NetDraw instructions are given below). There are four basic principles to constructing a sociograph that we will want our algorithms to follow:

1.   Points with the most ties should be near the center of the graph.
2.   Points adjacent to one another should be drawn in closer proximity than points that are more distant.
3.   Points with more common partners should be drawn in closer proximity than points with fewer common partners.
4.   The crossing of lines should be kept to a minimum and avoided whenever possible.

Let's try to apply these principles to our communication and advice networks. We'll start with the undirected communication adjacency matrix we created in Chapter 6.

Undirected graphs
To apply principle 1, we need to find out who has the most ties. We therefore begin by adding a column that gives the total number of ties for each person, by summing across rows.

We see that Mari, Philip, Sam, and Sarah each have 3 ties, so they should all be placed as points near the center of the graph to start. We then draw in lines for any relations between these four central persons, as seen in Figure 7.1. Note that, for undirected graphs, we can either use double arrows on each line or simply leave off arrowheads entirely.

We can now see that Mari, Sam, and Sarah are all adjacent to each other, but Philip is adjacent only to Mari, so Philip should be further from the others than he is from Mari or the others are to each other (by principles 2 and 3). So, in the next sociograph, Figure 7.2, we move Phil down a bit and pull Mari in more toward the center.

Then we add Buddy, who is the next most central in terms of number of ties. Since his two ties are to Philip and Sarah, he should be placed between them, but positioned further from the center and away from the others to whom he is not adjacent. See Figure 7.3.

Table 7.1   Summing across rows

	Bob	Buddy	Mari	Martha	Philip	Sam	Sarah	Row total
Bob	0	0	0	0	0	1	0	1
Buddy	0	0	0	0	1	0	1	2
Mari	0	0	0	0	1	1	1	3
Martha	0	0	0	0	1	0	0	1
Philip	0	1	1	1	0	0	0	3
Sam	1	0	1	0	0	0	1	3
Sarah	0	1	1	0	0	1	0	3

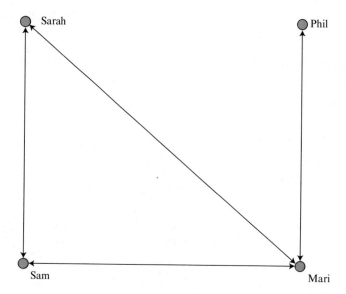

Figure 7.1   Starting an undirected sociograph

Notice that this requires that Philip and Sarah be to the same side of the graph. We happen to have placed them just so, by virtue of their alphabetical order, but this might not always work out so well.

Next, we can place Bob and Martha. Each has only one tie, so they should each be placed off to the side, away from the center, of the one person to whom they are adjacent, as in Figure 7.4.

There are no crossing lines, so this sociograph seems to meet our four criteria fairly well. However, it should be noted that this is by no means a unique solution: any number of other arrangements might meet the criteria just as well.

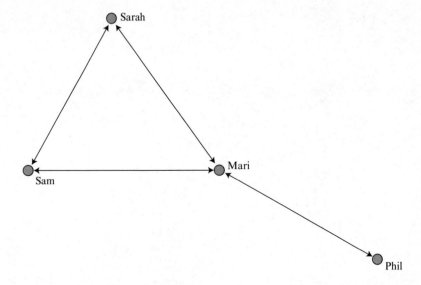

Figure 7.2   Adjusting an undirected sociograph

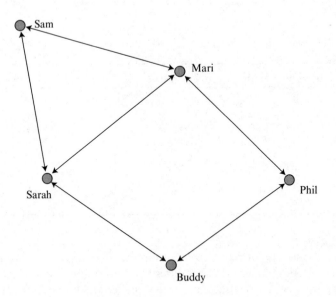

Figure 7.3   Constructing an undirected sociograph

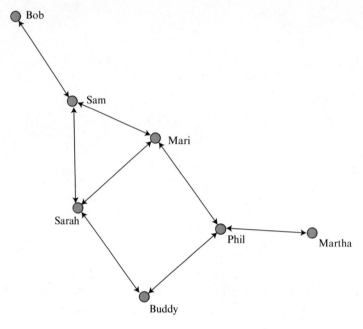

Figure 7.4   A completed undirected sociograph

Table 7.2   Summing across rows and down columns

	Bob	Buddy	Mari	Martha	Philip	Sam	Sarah	Out
Bob	0	0	1	0	0	1	0	2
Buddy	0	0	1	0	0	0	0	1
Mari	0	0	0	0	0	1	1	2
Martha	0	0	0	0	1	0	0	1
Philip	0	0	1	0	0	0	0	1
Sam	1	0	1	0	0	0	1	3
Sarah	0	0	1	0	0	1	0	2
In	1	0	5	0	1	3	2	

Directed graphs

Now, let's do our directed advice example. For directed relations, the number of 'goes to' ties may well differ from the number of 'comes to' ties. We refer to 'goes to' relations as out ties and 'comes to' relations as in ties. So, we form sums both across the rows for out and down the columns for in, and collect these as pairs, to make it easier to see who has the most ties, as in Tables 7.2 and 7.3.

Table 7.3   *Totalling ties*

	In	Out	Total
Bob	1	2	3
Buddy	0	1	1
Mari	5	2	7
Martha	0	1	1
Philip	1	1	2
Sam	3	3	6
Sarah	2	2	4

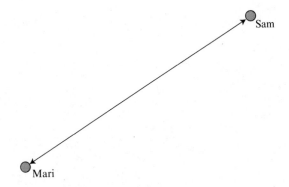

Figure 7.5   Starting a directed sociograph

We begin constructing the sociograph in Figure 7.5 by placing Mari and Sam in the center and drawing in the lines connecting them. Notice that, for directed relations, we put arrows on the lines indicating the direction of the relations.

In this case, Mari and Sam each seek advice from the other, so the arrow is double-headed. Then we add Sarah and Bob, connecting them to Sam and Mari in Figure 7.6. We see that we have a crossing of lines, which in this case highlights another violation: Bob and Sarah are as close to each other as they are to Mari and Sam, but yet they are not adjacent to each other, while each is tied to both Mari and Sam. This violates principles 2 and 3. We can fix all three violations by switching the positions of Sam and Bob and then pulling Bob out a bit and Sam in a bit, as shown in Figure 7.7.

This looks much better. It seems to adhere to all four principles. Again, this is not a unique solution. Applying the four principles is part science and part art. This is good enough to proceed. We add Phil in Figure 7.8.

Next, we need to add the final members, Martha and Buddy. Each has just one tie to the group and so they should be placed farther from the

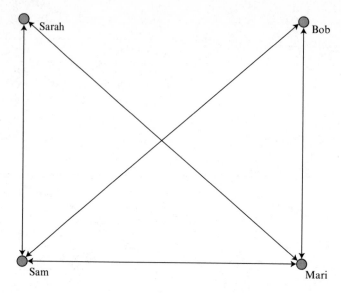

Figure 7.6   Placing nodes on a directed sociograph

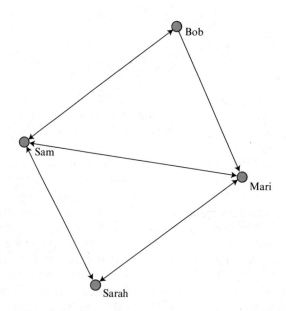

Figure 7.7   Adjusting a directed sociograph

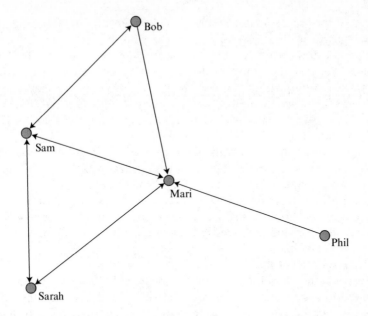

Figure 7.8   Continuing a directed sociograph

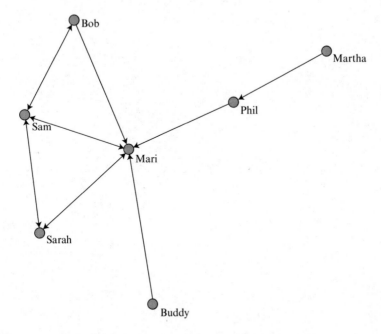

Figure 7.9   A final directed sociograph

center of the graph, as in Figure 7.9. This meets all four principles, and allows us to quickly see how each member is positioned.

Now, we don't really want to do this by hand, especially not for larger groups. So let's tell you how the graphs shown above were actually generated. We'll pick up here assuming you have correctly entered your networks into a spreadsheet editor and found a way to get the data into a computer network analysis and visualization package, such as NetDraw or Pajek.

Follow the commands for the package you're using to open and draw the graph. Doing so will result in a graph using default settings. If the graph looks good to you, then save the image. If you think it could be improved, look for a layout command which you can use to tell the program to apply our four rules. This will usually be called spring embedding or energy. You can also click on nodes and move them around by hand, if you wish.

7.3 Visualizing attributes

We can add the formal structure to the sociograph. We do so in our optics firm example by using division as an attribute and 'coloring' the nodes. Find the appropriate command in your software, select the attribute of division, and assign a unique shape to each division. If we do so, our graph

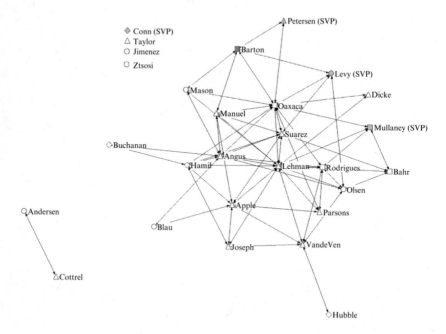

Figure 7.10   Optics firm trust sociograph, incorporating attribute data

now looks like Figure 7.10. The Mirror Lab, in shaded triangles, is clearly the central division, as we learned in Chapter 1. It is nice to have the visual confirmation.

See if you can reproduce the undergraduate cohort network we looked at earlier for the 'talk most' relation using the undergraduate cohort data. Load the data into a software package for network visualization. Doing so may instantly yield the graph from section 1.4, Figure 1.6. Or it could yield something rather messy.

If the nodes are all stacked to one side or seem strewn about at random, the program has not yet applied our principles. Tell it to do so by choosing a different layout algorithm. We can also get a clearer look at the structure by hiding the node labels. Depending on your system and sense of style, you may want to change the color or shape of the nodes.

For now, we want to recolor the nodes in our sociograph by gender. To reproduce Figure 1.6, select circles for women and squares for men. Also, change the color to light gray for women and dark gray for men. Note that you can choose other colors if you wish, rather than being constrained to the grayscale used here.

This ends our discussion of obtaining, preparing, and processing network data. We have covered how to construct and administer a network survey, enter and cross-check relational responses, convert individual responses into dyadic form, and obtain a network visualization. Having done all this with your data, you are likely eager to further analyze it. We will do so in Part III.

PART III

ANALYTIC METHODS

In this part, we present terminology, measures, and algorithms for performing a social network analysis in order to understand the social capital of a group or organization.

8 Analyzing structure

This chapter presents measures of the social structure of a network. The structure, as we have seen, is a key determinant of the amounts and types of social capital that members of the group or organization can tap into. Further, measures of structure will help to locate where social capital resides.

8.1 Global measures

Let us add some new terminology. A *complete* graph is one in which all of the points are adjacent to one another: each point is connected directly to every other point. The *density* of a graph is the actual number of ties which are present, in comparison to the total number of ties which would be present if the graph were complete. In other words, density measures the percentage of pairs of persons who are tied by the social relation defining the graph. Note that density differs from the number of points that are included in any lines (or relations), which in comparison to the total number of points is referred to as the *inclusiveness* of the graph. Density is a measure of overall tie activity, rather than node participation.

For an *undirected* graph, to get the number of ties we count the actual number of lines which are present in the sociograph. We could also get this by summing the upper triangular entries (above the diagonal) in the adjacency matrix. We then compare this count to the total number of lines which would be present if the graph were complete. For any undirected graph with n points, the number of lines in a complete graph is $n(n-1)/2$.

For *directed* graphs, computation of density is the number of arrows which are present, in comparison to the total number of arrows that would be present if the graph were complete in both directions. For a directed graph with n points, the number of arrows present in a complete graph in both directions is $n(n-1)$. From the adjacency matrix, we'd sum over all entries and divide by this number of permutations.

We can also characterize the graph by its *transitivity*. Three persons, A, B, and C, taken from a graph are transitive if, whenever person A is connected to person B and person B is connected to person C, person A is connected to person C. The density of transitive triples is the number of triples which are transitive divided by the number of paths of length 2, that is, the number of triples which have the potential to be transitive. The computation of transitivity works well as a measure of cohesion in undirected relations and as a measure of redundancy in directed relations.

We can also distinguish between global (or sociocentric) density and egocentric density. Global density is the density among all points in a graph, which is what we have been discussing so far. Egocentric density is the density among a person's direct contacts, once that focal person is removed. We'll focus on global density in this chapter. We'll pick the concept of egocentric density back up in Chapter 9.

Undirected

For our undirected communication network, we have seven persons, so there are (7*6)/2=21 possible pairwise relations. Of these, eight were observed (count the lines in the sociograph: [Bob, Sam], [Sam, Sarah], [Sam, Mari], [Sarah, Mari], [Sarah, Buddy], [Mari, Phil], [Phil, Buddy], and [Martha, Buddy]). So the density, expressed as a percentage, is 8/21*100=38.10%. In general, since density has a range from 1 to 100%, this is a moderately dense network. Whether that density indicates a problem or a well-functioning group depends on the formal organization and workflow involved. Notice that the inclusiveness of the graph, by contrast, is 100% (each person is involved in at least one relation).

The computation of transitivity requires some record keeping. We

Table 8.1   Undirected transitivity computation

Line=nodeA> nodeB	NodeA>nodeC	NodeB>nodeC	Transitive triple?
Bob, Sam	None	Sam>Sarah Sam>Mari	None
Sam, Sarah	Sam>Bob Sam>Mari	Sarah>Buddy Sarah>Mari	Sam, Mari, Sarah
Sam, Mari	Sam>Bob Sam>Sarah	Mari>Sarah Mari>Phil	Sam, Sarah, Mari
Sarah, Mari	Sarah>Sam Sarah>Buddy	Mari>Sam Mari>Phil	Sarah, Mari, Sam
Sarah, Buddy	Sarah>Sam Sarah>Mari	Buddy>Phil Buddy>Martha	None
Mari, Phil	Mari>Sam Mari>Sarah	Phil>Buddy	None
Phil, Buddy	Phil>Mari	Buddy>Sarah Buddy>Martha	None
Martha, Buddy	None	Buddy>Phil Buddy>Martha	None

need to get the denominator, which is the number of triples that have the potential to be transitive. The potential to be transitive stems from having the first two legs complete: A>B and B>C. Then our numerator comes by looking to see how many of those are transitive, with A>C. What this means is that we need to look at all the lines we just identified when computing density, and set the nodes off in pairs.

How many triples have the potential to be transitive? You should count 26. You'll find this by counting the number of lines A>B that also have an entry in the second column A>C or the third column, counting each such entry. We get our numerator by looking at the number of these that lead to an entry in the final column. You should be able to count six. Since this relation is undirected, there is really just one transitive triple, Sam, Sarah, and Mari, but the formula requires us to consider the six possible orders that you can impose on any group of three: (ABC), (ACB), (BAC), (BCA), (CAB), (CBA). Transitivity is then computed as 6/26=23%.

Directed

For our directed advice network, with seven persons there are (7*6)/2=21 possible pairs, but each pair can have two relations, one in each direction, so there are 42 possible pairwise relations. Counting the arrows in the sociograph, we find that 12 of these were actually observed. So the density, as a percentage, is 12/42*100=28.57%. Again, notice that the inclusiveness is 100%.

Transitivity follows the same template as we used for our communication example. We begin by tabulating the 12 lines observed, as in Table 8.2.

Our denominator, the number of triples with potential to be transitive, is just the count of entries in column 3 only (now being concerned with direction). We have enumerated 18 pairs in column 3 to match up the lines in column 1, forming triples in which A>B and B>C. Then our numerator is the count of entries in column 4, which complete the triple with an A>C line from column 2. Looking at column 4, we have enumerated nine such transitive triples. Our measure of transitivity is thus 9/18 = 50%.

Let's look at the trust network from the optics example in Chapter 1. Recall that our structural measures of social capital in general are density and transitivity. We further get at strong tie structure using both membership in and overlap of cliques. Choose Network>Cohesion>Density>Overall Density and browse to the input dataset; then click OK. All we need is the density from output log.

This density is 16.67%, which for a group of this size is considered moderate, although on the low end of that range. There is, thus, a limited amount of social capital available overall. While the potential for social

Table 8.2   Computing directed transitivity

Line=nodeA>nodeB	NodeA>nodeC	NodeB>nodeC	Transitive triple?
Bob>Sam	Bob>Mari	Sam>Mari Sam>Sarah	Bob>Sam>Mari
Bob>Mari	Bob>Sam	Mari>Sam Mari>Sarah	Bob>Mari>Sam
Buddy>Mari	None	Mari>Sam Mari>Sarah	None
Mari>Sam	Mari>Sarah	Sam>Sarah Sam>Bob	Mari>Sam>Sarah
Mari>Sarah	Mari>Sam	Sarah>Sam	Mari>Sarah>Sam
Martha>Phil	None	Phil>Mari	None
Phil>Mari	None	Mari>Sam Mari>Sarah	None
Sam>Bob	Sam>Mari Sam>Sarah	Bob>Mari	Sam>Bob>Mari
Sam>Mari	Sam>Sarah Sam>Bob	Mari>Sarah	Sam>Mari>Sarah
Sam>Sarah	Sam>Mari Sam>Bob	Sarah>Mari	Sam>Sarah>Mari
Sarah>Mari	Sarah>Sam	Mari>Sam	Sarah>Mari>Sam
Sarah>Sam	Sarah>Mari	Sam>Mari Sam>Bob	Sarah>Sam>Mari

capital may be moderate, it can still be quite valuable if distributed and used properly.

Transitivity of 39.90% tells us that, given the ties that exist, there is a moderate (high end) amount of redundancy, which is a building block of cohesion. Let's look more at the strong tie social capital, within this overall picture.

8.2   Subgraphs

We can also characterize a graph by its regions and subgroups. Besides being aware that the global structure has the contacts and cohesion captured in the overall measures of density and transitivity, we can locate where the attendant social capital resides in the structure. Cohesion exists where there is closure either in the full graph or in subparts of the graph, known as subgroups. Structural holes exist where lines are absent between nonequivalent regions. Subgroups and regions are both examples of subgraphs. We'll explain about subgraphs now.

Informal social relations often tie people into cohesive subgroups with their own norms, values, orientations, and cultures, which may run counter to the formal structures and policies of a group or organization. Cliques are among the most important sources of a person's identity and belonging, and can operate either to synergize individuals' efforts into a collective or to factionalize and divide members of the same formal group against one another.

We begin with the concept of a subgraph. A *subgraph* is a maximal collection of points selected from the whole graph of a network according to a defining characteristic, together with the lines connecting those points. By maximal, we mean that it is the largest collection of points that can be obtained without the defining characteristic disappearing.

8.2.1   Components

The simplest defining characteristic for a subgraph is that the points must all be connected, or linked to one another through paths. That is, all points must be able to reach each other through one or more paths, but have no connections outside the subgraph. Such a maximally connected subgraph is called a *component*. Within a component, all points are connected through paths, but no paths run to points outside the component. Components, in other words, are sets of points that link to one another through continuous chains of connection. By convention, we treat isolated points as each constituting a component.

For directed graphs, we can distinguish between strong components and weak components. A strong component is a component in which each point can reach every other point following a path in which the arrows line up tip to tail. A weak component is a component in which the direction of relations is ignored. Note that the use of the terms 'strong' and 'weak' here differs from that of strong and weak ties. Here, 'strong' simply means directed, whereas 'weak' means undirected.

With regard to components, if there are multiple components then there are parts of the network between which communication, advice, or support do not, and cannot, flow. Such a gap is one form of structural hole. Such gaps need to be carefully considered to determine if the lack of flow hinders organizational goals. It's worth investigating whether disjoint components are imploded, exploded, otherwise irregular, or properly functioning structures.

We can extend the concept of a component to find subgroups that are not strictly disjoint, but within which the connections are tighter than are the connections between groups. We call such groups k components, where k>1, but commonly refer to two components as *bicomponents*. Bicomponents are maximal collections of points for which each member must be able to reach each other member through at least two node-independent paths. Node independence requires that the nodes differ for the two paths. Bicomponents represent different, but not necessarily separate, parts of the network structure. Bicomponents can overlap, and if they do then the points of overlap represent key bridges (or potential bottlenecks) in the structure: they represent filled holes that may be fragile parts of the structure.

Let's take a look at the sociocentric structure of our director communication and advice networks. Beginning with the simple, undirected communication sociograph, we can find the components by asking whether each person can reach each of the others through a path of any length.

Let's build a list to keep track of things, anchored by the seven members of the entire network:

- Bob can reach Buddy through Sam and Sarah.
- Bob can reach Mari though Sam.
- Bob can reach Martha through Sam, Mari, and Phil.
- Bob can reach Phil though Sam and Mari.
- Bob can reach Sam directly.
- Finally, for Bob, he can reach Sarah through Sam.

Repeat for each of the others in the same manner.

What we find is that each member can reach every other member through a path of some length, so we have just a single component to our undirected communication network.

By inspection of the advice sociograph (Figure 7.9), we can see that there is a single undirected component to the advice network. That is, if we ignore the direction of the arrows, each person can reach every other person. Things are not so obvious when looking for directed components in the advice sociograph, so let's do the work. To find directed components, we need to ask whether each person can reach (get advice from) each other person. Notice that whether person A can reach person B through some path in which the arrows line up tip to tail and whether person B can reach person A through some, perhaps different, tip to tail path are not the same question.

Examination reveals that Bob, Mari, Sam, and Sarah can each reach each of the other three (Bob can reach Mari, Sam, and Sarah; Mari can reach Bob, Sam, and Sarah; Sam can reach Bob, Mari, and Sarah; and Sarah can reach Bob, Mari, and Sam). So one directed component consists of Bob, Mari, Sam, and Sarah. This is the main component: the remaining three persons are each isolated in the strong component sense (by convention, each is considered to be a component of one).

To better understand the implication of strong/directed components, let's look at Phil. Phil can reach Bob, Mari, Sam, and Sarah, each of the members of our main component. But, since none of them can reach Phil, he is not in the main component with them. This occurs because Phil seeks advice from Mari, but Mari does not seek Phil's advice. As a result, Bob, Sam, and Sarah cannot (or do not) get any advice from Phil either. The implication is that Phil can get information held by any member of the main component, via Mari, but they will not get information that he may have.

The advantage of looking at components with the directed/strong definition is that we can better differentiate between parts of the structure that are, in fact, different (some may be sources while others are sinks). The disadvantage is that we ignore the potential for a relation in one direction to be appropriated in the reverse direction. If an understanding of the latter is important, then we can analyze undirected/weak components, even if a relation is itself directed.

8.2.2 Bicomponents

In terms of bicomponents, examination of the communication sociograph reveals that Sam, Sarah, Buddy, Phil, and Mari are the main bicomponent. To form the bicomponent, we ask for each pair whether there are at least two paths, which differ by at least one intermediary, between the pair. We could keep track of this using a table just as we did for components. For example, Sam can reach Sarah directly or through Mari. These two paths differ in that Mari is in the latter, but not the former. Sam can reach Buddy through Sarah or through Mari and Phil. We can repeat this logic to verify the main bicomponent.

The convention for bicomponents is to define any connected dyads that are not within any other bicomponent to be their own bicomponent. In network terminology, a person with just a single tie into a component is known as a pendant (resembling a pendant hanging from a string). In this jargon, pendants and their connection to the component become defined as a bicomponent. So here we have Bob and Sam as a bicomponent and we have Martha and Phil as a bicomponent. No bicomponent can consist of fewer than two persons.

Any members that are in multiple bicomponents are by definition bridges (or potential bottlenecks). Here, Phil and Sam are bridges. To the extent that the bicomponents are bridged by a single member (or small minority of members), the structure may be fragile.

For directed relations, bicomponents are typically analyzed only in the undirected/weak sense. Hence, for our directed advice network, we would find a main bicomponent, consisting of Bob, Mari, Sam, and Sarah (verify that each can reach each of the others through at least two node-independent paths), and three pendant dyads: Mari and Phil, Mari and Buddy, and Phil and Martha. Mari bridges three subgroups, while Phil is a secondary bridge.

8.2.3   Cliques

A *clique* is defined as a maximally complete subgraph. Recall that a graph is complete when all points are adjacent (or directly tied to) all other points. Similarly, a subgraph is complete when all points in the subgraph are adjacent to all other points in the subgraph. Notice the difference between a component and a clique. In a component, all points must be able to reach all other points through paths of any length. In a clique, all points must be directly tied by a path of length 1 to all other points. For cliques, the direction of relations is always ignored. A clique is maximal if it is not contained in any other clique.

A maximally complete subgraph may also be referred to as a 1 clique, because each point must be tied to all other points at a path length of 1. We can loosen the definition so that all members must be connected by a maximum path length of 2, and refer to the resulting subgraph as a 2 clique. Of course, we could extend this reasoning to define 3 cliques and so forth, but path lengths greater than 2 involve rather more distant and weak ties. While an analysis of such weak ties might be interesting for some purposes, it is not at all clear that they get at our intuitive concept of a clique or subgroup. So we'll stick with defining just 1 cliques and 2 cliques. (Notice also that, if there are k persons in a subgroup, a k−1 clique is also a component.)

It is sometimes useful, if working with 2 cliques, to impose the additional restriction that the path distance between the most distant members (called the diameter of the clique) must be no greater than 2. In this case, we refer to the subgraph as a 2 clan. This is equivalent to saying that all points in the 2 clique must be connected to all others by a path distance of 2 or less through other members of the clique (so, for a clan, no paths through non-members of the subgraph are used in determining membership).

We can also loosen the definition of cliques by requiring each member to be directly connected to only n−k others (where n is the size of the subgraph), rather than requiring that they be connected to all others. We refer to such a subgraph as a k plex of the network (note that a clique is a 1 plex).

Once we have the cliques or other clique-like cohesive subgroups identified, we can look to see if the clique structures bring cohesion to the overall structure or result in fragmentation, by examining whether the cliques overlap and to what extent they follow departmental, rank, or other (e.g. gender, ethnicity) lines.

Keeping in mind that cliques are defined ignoring the direction, if any, of relations, let's look for cliques in our sociographs. We are looking for groups of persons who are each tied directly to each other, and for which we cannot find anyone else tied directly to each.

We can start with our communication sociograph. We could go back to our adjacency matrix, which shows who is directly tied to whom, but in this small network we can quickly see by inspection that Mari, Sam, and Sarah are each tied directly to each of the others. These three are a clique only if there is no one else who is directly tied to each of the three of them.

- Bob is directly tied only to Sam.
- Phil is tied directly only to Mari.
- Buddy and Martha are not directly tied to any of the three members of our would-be clique.

As a result, Sam, Mari, and Sarah are indeed a clique. It is common to look only for cliques of at least three persons, in which case we have found the only clique in the communication network.

Let's loosen the definition of a clique and look for 2 cliques in our communication network. Since Mari, Sam, and Sarah are a clique, they will all be in a 2 clique (if they are directly connected by a path of length 1, then they are also connected by a path of length less than 2), but they are not a 2 clique by themselves if we can find anyone else who is tied to each of them by paths of length 2 or less.

Look at Bob. Bob is tied directly to Sam, and through Sam is tied to Sarah and Mari each by paths of length 2.

Similarly, Buddy is tied directly to Sarah and through Sarah is tied to Mari and Sam by paths of length 2.

Phil is tied directly to Mari and through her to Sarah and Sam by paths of length 2.

It may be tempting to add Sam, Buddy, and Phil and think you have a 2 clique of six members. But look again. While Sam, Buddy, and Phil are each tied to Mari, Sam, and Sarah by paths of length less than 2, they are not all tied to each other by such short paths. Phil and Bob are three steps apart, as are Buddy and Bob.

Sam, Mari, Sarah, and Bob are a 2 clique, while Sam, Mari, Sarah, Buddy, and Phil are a different 2 clique. Martha is not in either of those 2 cliques, since she is three steps from Sarah and Sam. But Martha is in a 2 clique with Phil, Buddy, and Mari. Notice here that none of the paths connecting clique members goes outside of their cliques, so each clique is also a clan. Here, the process can be assisted by forming a new table that indicates for each pair the distance between them, allowing us to quickly find pairs that meet our looser criteria.

Let's look now for cliques in the directed advice network. While it is tempting to think our main component of Bob, Mari, Sam, and Sarah is a clique, this is not so. Notice that Sarah and Bob are not directly connected, so they cannot be in the same clique. Cliques can overlap, so we can see that:

- Bob, Mari, and Sam form a clique; and
- Mari, Sam, and Sarah form a second clique.

If we restrict our search to cliques of three or more, then these are the only two cliques in the advice network. Notice now that Mari and Sam are both in both cliques. Hence they are sources of unification for the overall network.

Now, let's loosen our clique definition by saying that each member need only be tied to n−2 members of the clique.

Bob, Mari, Sam, and Sarah now form a 2 plex: Sam and Mari are tied to each of the others, while Bob and Sarah are each tied to two of the three others, though not to each other directly. But this loosening also allows other subgroups to emerge:

- Bob, Buddy, Mari;
- Bob, Mari, Phil;
- Buddy, Mari, Phil;
- Buddy, Mari, Sam;
- Buddy, Mari, Sarah;
- Mari, Martha, Phil;
- Mari, Phil, Sam;
- Mari, Phil, Sarah.

There is a great deal of overlap: Mari appears in every 2 plex, but she is not the only bridge, so the structure seems robust. This sort of proliferation often occurs as we loosen our definition, so we may want to restrict our attention to subgroups of larger size as we do so. Notice that, with k=2, there are eight 2 plexes of size 3, but only one of size 4.

When looking for cohesive subgroups, you should start by looking for garden-variety cliques. If you find any cliques here, you do not need to look for n cliques (e.g. 2 cliques) or k plexes. If you don't find any 1 cliques, then you can try loosening the definition by looking for 2 cliques or, failing any 2 cliques, looking for 2 plexes. If you do not find any of these, then you might conclude that the network does not have cohesive subgroups.

Let's see the cliques in the structure of the trust network for the optics firm. There are 23 cliques found:

1. Oaxaca, Lehman, Angus, Suarez, Manuel;
2. Oaxaca, Lehman, Angus, Suarez, Hamil;
3. Rodrigues, Oaxaca, Lehman, Angus;
4. Oaxaca, Lehman, Angus, Mason;
5. Mullaney (SVP), Rodrigues, Oaxaca, Lehman;
6. Rodrigues, Oaxaca, Lehman, Parsons;
7. Oaxaca, Lehman, Dicke;
8. Mullaney (SVP), Bahr, Lehman;
9. Bahr, Lehman, Suarez;
10. Bahr, Lehman, Olsen;
11. Lehman, Joseph, VandeVen, Apple;
12. Lehman, Joseph, Apple, Hamil;
13. Rodrigues, Lehman, VandeVen, Olsen;
14. Lehman, Suarez, Manuel, Apple;
15. Lehman, Suarez, Apple, Hamil;
16. Lehman, Parsons, Apple;
17. Rodrigues, Lehman, Angus, Olsen;
18. Barton, Petersen (SVP), Oaxaca;
19. Barton, Levy (SVP), Oaxaca;
20. Levy (SVP), Oaxaca, Suarez;
21. Barton, Oaxaca, Manuel;
22. Barton, Oaxaca, Mason;
23. Angus, Buchanan, Hamil.

There is definitely some strong tie social capital in this network indicated by the 23 cliques with overlapping membership. Cottrel appears in no cliques whatsoever. He has no strong tie social capital, as we measure it. Notice that Lehman, the choice to co-chair the task force, appears in 17 of the 23 cliques.

You should also be able to see here why we asked about Petersen back in Chapter 1. As head of the Mirror Lab, he is in only one clique and not with members of his division. That indicates a leadership concern, with Angus in six cliques of mixed divisional composition a clear candidate to succeed Petersen. Doing so may not only help internal issues in the Mirror Lab but also help in resolving the conflict between the Mirror Lab and the other divisions.

Looking at components and bicomponents gives a sense of the weak tie social capital available, within the overall structure. Doing this for the optics firm gives the following. First are the components. There are six components, but only two consist of non-isolates. There is one main component, with 22 workers, and then a small component made up of Cottrel and Andersen. The number of isolates indicates that there is opportunity for more weak tie social capital to be developed. To get a sense of how much currently exists, we look at bicomponents.

Six components are found:

Component	Nodes	Proportion
1	22	0.786
2	1	0.036
3	2	0.071
4	1	0.036
5	1	0.036
6	1	0.036

Three blocks are found:

- Block 1: VandeVen, Hubble;
- Block 2: Barton, Petersen (SVP), Bahr, Rodrigues, Oaxaca, Lehman, Angus, Joseph, Dicke, Suarez, VandeVen, Manuel, Apple, Blau, Olsen, Buchanan, Hamil;
- Block 3: Cottrel, Andersen.

Four blocks are found:

- Block 1: Blau;
- Block 2: Cottrel, Suarez;
- Block 3: Cottrel, Andersen;
- Block 4: Barton, Petersen (SVP), Bahr, Oaxaca, Cottrel, Lehman, Angus, Joseph, Dicke, Taylor, VandeVen, Manuel, Apple, Jimenez, Olsen, Zstosi, Hubble, Buchanan, Hamil.

Here, a block is a bicomponent and there are three. This suggests that there is not much weak tie social capital in this structure as it currently stands. Now, we should point out that this is a trust network, so it may well be that weak tie social capital is not critical. Given the nature of trust, strong tie social capital is a closer relative.

Switching to the advice network, we would typically like to see more weak tie social capital. The bicomponents are shown in the output log. There is a tad more weak tie social capital, but there does seem to be a concern here, as much of it is concentrated around one person.

Let's also look at the cliques and components for the undergraduate cohort data. There are 85 cliques among the 89 students who actually make up the cohort.

85 cliques are found:

1. 1000, 1235, 1247, 1512;
2. 1000, 1235, 1481, 1512;
3. 1000, 1440, 1481, 1512;
4. 1000, 1496, 1512;
5. 1000, 1016, 1066, 1254;
6. 1000, 1012, 1016, 1066;
7. 1000, 1104, 1240;
8. 1000, 1104, 1304;
9. 1000, 1104, 1496;
10. 1000, 1118, 1235, 1247;
11. 1000, 1158, 1194, 1240;
12. 1000, 1158, 1248;
13. 1000, 1012, 1248;
14. 1000, 1345, 1440, 1481 . . . (more output suppressed).

Blocks found are:

- Block 1: 1227, 1469;
- Block 2: 1478, 1489;
- Block 3: 1065, 1402;
- Block 4: 1065, 1571;
- Block 5: 1065, 1594;
- Block 6: 1013, 1442;
- Block 7: 1518, 1566;
- Block 8: 1000, 1009, 1011, 1012, 1013, 1016, 1022, 1023, 1035, 1066, 1081, 1084, 1088, 1089, 1093, 1098, 1100, 1104, 1118, 1139, 1158, 1159, 1173, 1183, 1187, 1194, 1201, 1216, 1218, 1232, 1234, 1235, 1240, 1247, 1248, 1249, 1252, 1253, 1254, 1255, 1281, 1287, 1304, 1312, 1314, 1316, 1321, 1345, 1347, 1348, 1394, 1399, 1404, 1409, 1426, 1440, 1466, 1469, 1476, 1479, 1481, 1489, 1496, 1497, 1511, 1512, 1520, 1521, 1525, 1533, 1537, 1554, 1558, 1561, 1566, 1594, 1606, 1607, 1615;
- Block 9: 1327, 1458, 1586.

There is certainly some strong tie social capital. Most of the cliques are small, with just three students each, but there is quite a bit of overlap. The result of these two factors is that the strong tie social capital is concentrated around 10–15 students.

Turning to weak tie structure, we find just nine bicomponents, with one main group, one three-person group, and seven pendants. This is a relatively sparse bicomponent structure for such a large network, suggesting a potential deficiency in weak tie social capital.

8.3   Small worlds

The concept of *small worlds* has garnered a lot of media attention in the past decade and been the subject of renewed scholarly interest. Duncan Watts (1999) is principally credited with the scholarly revival, having published a number of books and articles on the subject. As he relates, 'you have probably had the experience of meeting a complete stranger with whom [you] have apparently little in common and finding unexpectedly that [you] share a mutual acquaintance', leading you to exclaim 'It's a small world.'

The notion of a small world is captured in the story of an experiment conducted in the 1960s. An investigator gave a variety of subjects items and asked them to forward them to a group of prominent individuals. The catch was that the subjects had to deliver them to someone they knew personally, by first name, and so forth. In the end, the average number of intermediaries needed to get the items delivered was six: hence the now famous phrase 'six degrees of separation'.

That story itself misses some important details that make the world less small than it at first appeared. Most telling, only about 40 percent of the items made it to their destination at all. It seems that 60 percent of the world is actually quite large. That aside, more recent work has demonstrated the existence of small worlds in a number of fields from the world wide web to industrial networks. What is a small world, then?

Watts lays out four criteria for us to experience the small world phenomenon:

1. The world has to actually be large, in terms of the number of nodes. Otherwise we would not be surprised by our common acquaintances.
2. The network must be sparse overall, in that each node is connected to only a few, say k, other nodes on average, where $k<<n$.
3. The network must not be centralized, that is, there should be no node with a degree close to n.
4. The network must be clustered, that is, there must be overlapping social circles in which many of our friends are also friends.

These criteria combine to capture the sense we have of being part of a small world. Analyzing small worlds, however, requires formalization of measures that can distinguish a small world structure from other structures that are otherwise similar.

Watts identified two features that set small world networks apart from others: short average paths and a high degree of local clustering. Let's say more about these and how they can be measured.

The *characteristic path length* (CPL) of a network refers to the average distance between any two nodes. The path length can be thought of as the degree of separation, although the term 'degree' is used differently here than we have otherwise defined it. In a social network, it is simply the number of intermediaries you have to go through to reach any other person.

The *clustering coefficient* (CC) measures the extent of local density, that is, whether there are actors around whom there is more activity, with a great many ties among their alters, while other ego networks have fewer ties. When this is the case, we'd say there is a high degree of clustering around the popular actors. We'd also tend to describe a popular node as a hub, around which much of the activity of the network flows. Formally, the cluster coefficient is the average local density of an ego network (ignoring ties to ego), taken over all egos. As Watts notes, this can also be interpreted as the probability that any two nodes will be connected, given that they share a mutual friend.

Small worlds is a relative concept, so that a comparison needs to be made to a network that is similar in total size, average degree, and connectivity. To find such a comparison in practice would be confounded by other differences, so we generate a random network with the same comparison parameters.

Small worlds is a concept that applies only to large-scale networks. So we'll use the undergraduate cohort as an example. Is the cohort a small world? We can begin by visually comparing a contrived small world to the sociograph for the undergraduate cohort.

To construct a small world, Watts first draws something called a *connected caveman* network, representing the case of a large, highly clustered graph.

This graph, shown upper left in Figure 8.1, however, has a rather large characteristic path length, and so does not qualify as a small world. This is because, in order to get to a cluster on the other side of the world, you have to walk all the way around, from one cluster to the next, until you reach your destination.

For a large graph with low CPL and fixed degree, Watts recommends a random graph with equal probability. Yet such a graph will not have much local clustering, so we need two bases of comparison to judge a potential small world against. It must have clustering of the same order as a connected caveman graph, while having short path lengths such as a random graph with equal probability, both of the same size and degree.

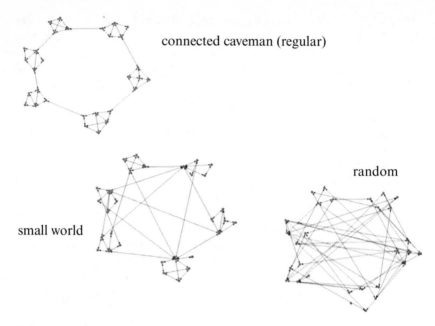

connected caveman (regular)

random

small world

Figure 8.1   Fitting in a small world

Figure 8.1 places a schematic of a small world network between the extremes of a regular (includes caveman) and a random network. Notice the cross-cutting ties that can be used to jump to the other side of the world, reducing the CPL.

It may seem difficult to make a visual comparison between such stylized schematics and an actual large-scale network such as our undergraduate cohort. Yet we simply need to identify the hallmarks to look for. In the small world, we see distinct local neighborhoods or regions that are connected by cross-cutting ties. Now, let's turn to the sociograph for the undergraduate cohort (refer to Figure 1.6).

There are two clear regions with local density that are connected by just a few cross-cutting ties. But it seems likely that the size of the regions is too large as portions of the overall graph for this to be a small world. Still, let's go through the exercise of seeing how it stacks up against regular and random networks with the same size and degree.

We'll first get the characteristic path length (CPL) and clustering coefficient (CC) for the undergraduate sociograph. The clustering coefficient is .487 and the average distance, or path length, is 3.269.

Now, let's rewire the network to maximize the clustering coefficient, given the size of the group and number and aggregate distribution of ties.

Assuming you can find the commands to do so in your software package, the clustering coefficient and characteristic path length will be in the ball-park of CC=.771 and the CPL=2.431. Your numbers may not be exactly the same, since the rewiring has a random element to it. The general result, in terms of how the CC and CPL compare to the original matrix, should be about the same.

Interestingly, increasing the CC has also reduced the CPL, making the result more of a small world than our actual graph. Before concluding, we need to see what a network with the same size and degree is capable of in terms of the CPL. Rewire again, this time choosing to minimize the distances. The clustering coefficient for the random rewiring in constructing this example is now 0.465 and the average distance, or CPL, is 1.931.

The closest this graph could get to being a small world, then, would be to have a CC ~0.771 and a CPL ~1.931. Our undergraduate cohort is not really a small world. This is due, mostly, to the relatively large size of the clustered regions. To be a small world, there would need to be more local clusters, each smaller in size.

Before we go, we should answer an obvious, but so far overlooked, question: why would you want to know if a network is a small world? A small world is a network in which those you might not expect to bump into one another may just do so or their information and resources may bump without them, as they may have common friends in spite of their separation in the social structure. As a result, news from one department or division may not remain isolated. As a manager, you would want to treat them equitably, and use care in disclosing information and allocating resources.

Beyond that, a small world is a structure that contains more social capital than might otherwise be thought, since a formative basis for a social tie exists whenever there are common partners. Members of a small world may, thus, find they have social capital in unexpected places.

8.4 Formative bases

Our understanding of the network structure can help us to diagnose problems or identify opportunities in organizations. From a practical standpoint, if a problem is diagnosed, we need to understand the social processes by which relations formed in order to formulate and enact a solution. If the social structure appears to be operating in a functional way for the organization, we may also benefit from understanding the formative social processes. Identifying processes that lead to well-functioning structures can assist us in creating new structures or altering other poorly functioning groups.

In particular, we are interested in identifying individual characteristics that might drive homophily or heterophily. Homophily was defined as the process by which those with similar characteristics are drawn together in relations. Heterophily, by contrast, describes when dissimilar persons have social relations. Although homophily is considered a general, naturally occurring social process, heterophily often occurs by design (as when persons from different departments are assigned together on a team). To look for homophily or heterophily, we need to examine the similarity or dissimilarity along individual characteristics among dyads that have a social relation (of a given type or types) as compared to dyads that are not so tied.

We do so by regressing the relational data on the transformed attribute/affiliation data. More specifically, we perform a QAP regression in which an adjacency matrix for a social relation is the dependent variable, and any number of attribute/affiliation dyadic similarity or dissimilarity matrices are independent variables. The QAP regression will provide coefficients giving the slope of a linear relationship between the independent variables and the dependent social tie. The regression will also give us the significance level of the coefficient estimate. Recall two things. First, regression coefficients are interpreted as the amount of change in the dependent variable that is estimated to result from a unit increase in the independent variable. Second, coefficients are interpreted as such only if they are significant. Recall also that a result is significant only if the significance level falls below a predetermined, small value, such as .05.

If the independent variable is a similarity matrix, a significant positive coefficient indicates that greater similarity makes a tie more likely. Alternatively, if the independent variable is a dissimilarity matrix, a significant negative coefficient would indicate that greater dissimilarity makes the tie less likely, which implies that similarity makes it more likely. These cases provide evidence for homophily.

Heterophily is evident in either of the two alternative cases: the independent variable is a similarity matrix and the coefficient is significant and negative, or the independent variable is a dissimilarity matrix and the coefficient is significant and positive.

You can implement the statistical test in UCINET, Pajek, or other available software packages; just choose QAP or dyadic regression. Enter an adjacency matrix as the dependent variable and enter as many of the similarity/dissimilarity matrices as you wish for independent variables.

Working concrete examples will make more sense. In the board of directors example, we'll first look for homophily/heterophily in our communication network based on age, gender, aptitude, and community organization membership. Here are the results:

Regression coefficients

Independent	Unstandardized coefficient	Standardized coefficient	Significance	Proportions	
				As large	As small
Intercept	0.910603	0.000000	0.101	0.101	0.899
ORGSIM	0.151832	0.242822	0.143	0.143	0.857
APTDIF	0.128626	0.165048	0.235	0.766	0.235
AGEDIF	−0.051755	−0.525350	0.005	0.996	0.005
SEXSIM	0.051867	0.052855	0.427	0.427	0.573

While QAP regression works a bit differently than the ordinary least squares regression you are probably most familiar with, we read the QAP regression output very much like any other kind of regression. We can look at the significance levels for each of the similarity/dissimilarity matrices and see that AGEDIF is significant at the .05 level. The sign on AGEDIF is negative, indicating that those who are different in age are less likely to be tied in communication relations. Hence, those who are similar in age are more likely to communicate. This is evidence for age homophily as one basis for our communication network.

Regression coefficients

Independent	Unstandardized coefficient	Standardized coefficient	Significance	Proportions	
				As large	As small
Intercept	0.567649	0.000000	0.264	0.264	0.736
ORGSIM	0.067132	0.115411	0.293	0.293	0.707
APTDIF	−0.003902	−0.005382	0.436	0.436	0.564
AGEDIF	−0.038844	−0.423853	0.036	0.964	0.036
SEXSIM	0.027172	0.029765	0.472	0.528	0.472

Turning to the advice network, we simply change the dependent variable and rerun the QAP regression to get the output. Again, we find evidence for age homophily as a driving force. Finally, is there age homophily in trust? Simply change the dependent variable and rerun the QAP regression to find out. There is evidence for age homophily in trust, but we also find that trust forms between those who are similar in aptitude as well.

Regression coefficients

Independent	Unstan-dardized coefficient	Standard-ized coefficient	Signifi-cance	Proportions	
				As large	As small
Intercept	1.037402	0.000000	0.006	0.006	0.994
ORGSIM	0.008793	0.015531	0.478	0.522	0.478
APTDIF	−0.281718	−0.399271	0.012	0.988	0.012
AGEDIF	−0.039963	−0.448054	0.008	0.992	0.008
SEXSIM	0.122976	0.138416	0.23	0.239	0.761

We can use the data on level and division along with the trust adjacency matrix to conduct tests for homophily in the optics firm example. Pick the trust adjacency matrix for the dependent variable and select both the level difference and division match matrices as independent variables. What do you conclude about tie formation in the optics company based on this output?

Regression coefficients

Independent	Unstan-dardized coefficient	Standard-ized coefficient	Signifi-cance	Proportions	
				As large	As small
Intercept	0.164079	0.000000			
Level	−0.048555	−0.077761	0.216	0.784	0.216
Division	0.079525	0.09382	0.066	0.066	0.934

A variety of additional measures is available for the undergraduate cohort data from Koput and Gutek (in press). Imagine we would like to know whether there is gender-based homophily and whether students form natural groups based on grades.

Using the demographic data for the cohort, we can convert gender into a similarity matrix using the match rule. For grades, GPA is a numerical variable, so we can use absolute differences.

Then we can use the two matrices for gender match and grade differences as independent variables to predict 'talk most' ties. Examining the regression coefficients below, which is/are important: gender or grades? More important? Is there evidence for homophily or something else?

Regression coefficients

Independent	Unstan-dardized coefficient	Standard-ized coefficient	Signifi-cance	Proportions	
				As large	As small
Intercept	0.035882	0.000000			
Gender	0.050174	0.110251	0.000	0.000	1.000
Grades	−0.012595	−0.028521	0.049	0.952	0.049

In this chapter, we covered methods for analyzing the global, or socio-centric, properties of a network. The associated measures give us a sense of the amount, types, and location of social capital in a formal organization. We can also assess the factors that underlie the formation and mainte-nance of social ties.

We next turn to methods for analyzing the social capital available to members based on their individual, or egocentric, positions in the social structure. When combined, the sociocentric and egocentric measures will give us a sense of who has how much social capital, of what type, and what they can do with it.

9 Analyzing positions

9.1 Centrality

Centrality, in general, is a property of points in a graph. Related to social capital, centrality can be used to measure the potential for access and control over information and resources. There are two conceptualizations of centrality of a point related to access: local and global. The measure of centrality related to control is often considered intermediate.

A point is locally central if it has a large number of connections with the other points if it has a large neighborhood of direct contacts. A point is globally central if it has a position of strategic significance in the overall structure of the network – if it can reach other points on short paths. Local centrality is concerned with the relative activity of a focal point (called ego) in its neighborhood (of alters), while global centrality concerns reach within the whole network.

9.1.1 Degree

The simplest and most straightforward measure of local centrality is called the degree of a point. The degree is simply the number of points to which a point is adjacent. A point is locally central if it has a high degree.

For an undirected graph, the degree of a point is just the number of lines that are attached to the point. Working from the adjacency matrix, you can obtain this by summing across the row for the point.

For directed graphs, we can distinguish between the number of lines with arrows coming in to the point (the InDegree, also the column sum of the adjacency matrix) and the number of lines with arrows going away from the point (the OutDegree, also the row sum). Separating InDegree from OutDegree can be useful in separating the key experts (advice givers) from those who are clueless (advice seekers).

When comparing graphs of different sizes, it is sometimes useful to normalize the degree measure. We do so by dividing degree by $(n-1)$ and then multiplying by 100, where n is the number of points in the graph.

9.1.2 Closeness

Our measure of global centrality is the closeness of a point. A point is close to another point if the distance between them (along the geodesic connecting them) is small. The sum of the distances between a point and all other points is called the farness of the focal point. A point with a low farness is close to a large number of other points, and so closeness is computed as the normalized reciprocal of farness. That is, closeness is measured by summing the distances between a point and all other points, dividing by (n−1), and then taking the reciprocal and multiplying by 100.

For undirected graphs, there is one distance connecting any pair of points along the geodesic(s). For directed graphs, there are two possible distances along geodesics in opposite directions between each pair of points: the shortest paths connecting them for which the arrows line up tip to tail going in each direction (e.g. from point A out to B versus from point B in to A). For directed graphs, then, we separately compute the InCloseness and the OutCloseness. For each point, InCloseness is computed by looking at the geodesics coming in to that point from each other point, whereas OutCloseness is computed by looking at the geodesics going out of that point to each other point.

Note that, if there is no path connecting two points, as when they are in different components, there is no geodesic between them and the distance is theoretically not defined. In practice, it has become conventional to set the distance for such pairs to equal the size of the group, N, which is one step greater than the longest possible distance between points that are connected by any path(s) in a group of size N.

9.1.3 Betweenness

The betweenness of a point measures the extent to which a person can play the part of a broker or gatekeeper. That is, betweenness measures (potential) control over the flow of information and resources in a network. Although intuitive, betweenness is the most complex of the measures of point centrality to calculate.

The betweenness proportion of a focal point is defined for each pair of other points as the proportion of geodesics connecting the other points which pass through the focal point.

The betweenness score of the point is then found by combining all such betweenness proportions involving the focal point. Betweenness can be normalized by dividing the betweenness score by the factor [(n−1)*(n−2)/2] and multiplying by 100.

For undirected graphs, a geodesic is the shortest path connecting a pair of points and runs symmetrically in both directions. For directed graphs, a geodesic between each pair of other points is a path of shortest length for which the arrows line up tip to tail. But each pair can have two geodesics, as the geodesic running from A to B is a separate path from the geodesic running from B to A. The betweenness score for each point is computed

Table 9.1   Degree computation

Ego	Lines to	Degree (number of lines attached)
Bob	Sam	1
Buddy	Phil, Sarah	2
Mari	Phil, Sam, Sarah	3
Martha	Phil	1
Phil	Buddy, Mari, Martha	3
Sam	Bob, Mari, Sarah	3
Sarah	Buddy, Mari, Sam	3

as before but summed over all $[(n-1)*(n-2)]$ geodesics. This betweenness would then be normalized by dividing by $[(n-1)*(n-2)]$ and multiplying by 100.

9.1.4   Examples

Undirected centrality   Let's work out each of the centrality measures of our fictive group of seven: Bob, Buddy, Mari, Martha, Phil, Sam, and Sarah. We'll start with the simpler, undirected case using the communication network.

To compute degree centrality for each person, we simply count the number of direct ties they have: the number of lines attached to their point. Table 9.1 keeps track of who each point is directly tied to, and then counts the lines.

Notice that the degree can also be obtained from Table 7.1 by summing across the row for each person. To see this, compare the degree measures in Table 9.1 to the row sums we computed in Table 7.1.

Closeness is a more difficult computation, involving the distance between the focal person and each other person. Recall that the distance is the length along the geodesic (shortest path). So, for each point, we must find the geodesic to each other point and then find the distance between the pair. We average the distances, invert, and multiply by 100 to get closeness. We can use Table 9.2 to keep track of the calculation.

Get the idea? If so, then you should be able to verify the complete closeness scores in Table 9.3.

Betweenness is even more laborious. For each person, we need to consider the geodesics for every pair of other points (not including the focal point, or ego).

For each point, there are $(n-1)*(n-2)/2$ pairs of other points.

Table 9.2   Closeness computation

Ego	Alter	Intermediaries on geodesic	Distance	Average distance	Closeness
Bob	Buddy	Sam>Sarah	3		
	Mari	Sam	2		
	Martha	Sam>Mari>Phil	4		
	Phil	Sam>Mari	3		
	Sam		1		
	Sarah	Sam	2	15/6=2.5	100/2.5=40
Buddy	Bob	Sarah>Sam	3		
	Mari	Sarah (or Phil)	2		
	Martha	Phil	2		
	Phil		1		
	Sam	Sarah	2		
	Sarah		1	11/6=1.833	100/1.83=54.5

Table 9.3   Closeness scores

Ego	Average distance	Closeness
Bob	2.5	40
Buddy	1.833	54.5
Mari	1.5	66.67
Martha	2.5	40
Phil	1.67	60
Sam	1.67	60
Sarah	1.67	60

For each of these pairs, we find all the geodesics (all the paths with the length of the shortest path).

Then we ask, for each geodesic, whether the ego is on the path.

We then convert this to the proportion of geodesics that the ego is on and sum over all pairs of other points (and normalize if we wish to compare across networks of different size).

Let's build Table 9.4 to show the calculation for Bob. There should be 6*5/2=15 pairs of others.

Table 9.4 indicates that Bob has no betweenness centrality. This should seem obvious in retrospect, as simple inspection of the sociograph shows that Bob is an endpoint, or pendant, and as such cannot be between others.

Let's look at Buddy in Table 9.5, as we can see by inspection of the sociograph that Buddy is not a pendant. Buddy has some, nonzero,

Table 9.4   Betweenness computation for Bob

Ego	Pair of others	Intermediaries on geodesic(s)	Is ego on geodesic?	Proportion on	Betweenness
Bob	Buddy, Mari	Sarah (or Phil)	N (N)	0	
	Buddy, Martha	Phil	N	0	
	Buddy, Phil		N	0	
	Buddy, Sam	Sarah	N	0	
	Buddy, Sarah		N	0	
	Mari, Martha	Phil	N	0	
	Mari, Phil		N	0	
	Mari, Sam		N	0	
	Mari, Sarah		N	0	
	Martha, Phil		N	0	
	Martha, Sam	Phil>Mari	N	0	
	Martha, Sarah	Phil>Mari (or Phil>Buddy)	N (N)	0	
	Phil, Sam	Mari	N	0	
	Phil, Sarah	Mari (or Buddy)	N (N)	0	
	Sam, Sarah		N	0	Sum=0

betweenness and thus some potential control. But is it much social capital? Table 9.5 shows how it stacks up.

See if you can verify the final betweenness scores in Table 9.6. We can conclude that Buddy has relatively little control compared to some of the others. Bob and Martha clearly have none, as expected for pendants. Notice that Phil has the most. Is this surprising? Who would you have expected, based on looking at the sociograph, to have had the most?

Directed centrality   Now let's take a look at how things get handled when we want to consider direction of a relation in our computation of centrality. We can use our directed advice network as an example.

Degree   Beginning with the simplest measure, degree, the key difference is that we now must attend to in relations separately from out relations. We do so by counting the arrows going into a point separately from those going out of a point. We could also do this by summing across rows and down columns of the adjacency matrix.

We can see, from the graph, that Bob has two arrows going out and only one coming in. This establishes his degree centrality. Let's build another table to keep track of things, Table 9.7.

Mari is clearly the expert, with the highest InDegree, while Martha

Table 9.5 Betweenness computation for Buddy

Ego	Pair of others	Intermediaries on geodesic(s)	Is ego on geodesic?	Proportion on	Betweenness
Buddy	Bob, Mari	Sam	N (N)	0	
	Bob, Martha	Sam>Mari>Phil	N	0	
	Bob, Phil	Sam>Mari	N	0	
	Bob, Sam		N	0	
	Bob, Sarah	Sam	N	0	
	Mari, Martha	Phil	N	0	
	Mari, Phil		N	0	
	Mari, Sam		N	0	
	Mari, Sarah		N	0	
	Martha, Phil		N	0	
	Martha, Sam	Phil>Mari	N	0	
	Martha, Sarah	Phil>Mari (or Phil>Buddy)	N (Y)	0.5	
	Phil, Sam	Mari	N	0	.5+.5=1
	Phil, Sarah	Mari (or Buddy)	N (Y)	0.5	100/15
	Sam, Sarah		N	0	=6.67

Table 9.6 Betweenness scores

Ego	Betweenness	Normalized betweenness
Bob	0	0
Buddy	1	6.67
Mari	5	33.33
Martha	0	0
Phil	5.5	36.67
Sam	5	33.33
Sarah	2.5	16.67

provides no advice. Sam gets the most advice, which might reflect being a novice, but importantly shows he has social capital sources to get the information he needs. Notice that Mari, our expert, nonetheless also seeks advice from others, and so provides and uses social capital.

Closeness Directed closeness is a more difficult computation, involving the distance between the focal person and each other person along a path in which the arrows line up tip to tail. Now the arrows can line up coming in to ego or they may line up going out from ego to the other. Hence, we

Table 9.7   Directed degree computation

Ego	Arrows in from	Arrows out to	InDegree (number of arrows in)	OutDegree (number of arrows out)
Bob	Sam	Mari, Sam	1	2
Buddy	Mari		1	0
Mari	Bob, Buddy, Phil, Sam, Sarah	Sam, Sarah	5	2
Martha		Phil	0	1
Phil	Martha	Mari	1	1
Sam	Bob, Mari, Sarah	Bob, Mari, Sarah	3	3
Sarah	Mari, Sam	Mari, Sam	2	2

must compute separate InCloseness and OutCloseness. For each point, we must find both the in-geodesic and the out-geodesic for each other point. Then, separately for in and out, we find the distance between the pair in the indicated direction, average the distances, invert, and multiply by 100 to get closeness. Refer to Table 9.8.

Get the idea? If so, then you should be able to verify the complete closeness table for directed advice relations in Table 9.9.

Here we see that Mari is the most well positioned to give advice, with Sam and then Sarah the next most globally central. There is not all that much variation in OutCloseness, suggesting that all of the members of the group do tap into the network for advice to an even extent.

Betweenness   Betweenness for directed relations is again even more laborious. Betweenness necessarily entails flows that go both in to and out of a point (otherwise, you wouldn't be in between; you'd just be a source or sink). So each point will have just a single betweenness score. But, for each point as ego, we need to consider the geodesics for every ordered pair of other points (not including the focal point, or ego).

For each point, there are $(n-1)*(n-2)/2$ pairs of other points, but each pair can have geodesics running in each direction, so there are $(n-1)*(n-2)$ ordered (or directed) pairs. For each ordered pair, we find all the geodesics (all the paths with the length of the shortest path). Then we ask, for each geodesic, whether the ego is on the geodesic. We then convert this to the proportion of geodesics that the ego is on and sum over all ordered pairs of other points (and normalize if we wish to compare across networks of different size). The calculation for Mari appears in Table 9.10. There should be 6*5=30 ordered pairs of others.

Table 9.8 Directed closeness computation

Ego	Alter	Intermediaries on in-geodesic	In-distance	InCloseness	Intermediaries on out-geodesic	Out-distance	OutCloseness
Mari	Bob		1		Sam	2	
	Buddy		1		No out-geo	7	
	Martha	Phil	2		No out-geo	7	
	Phil		1		No out-geo	7	
	Sam		1	6/7		1	6/25
	Sarah		1	*100		1	*100
			7	=85.71		25	=24
Martha	Bob	No in-geo	7		Phil>Mari>Sam	4	
	Buddy	No in-geo	7		No out-geo	7	
	Mari	No in-geo	7		Phil	2	
	Phil	No in-geo	7			1	
	Sam	No in-geo	7	6/42	Phil>Mari	3	6/20
	Sarah	No in-geo	7	*100	Phil>Mari	3	*100
			42	=14.29		20	=30

Table 9.9   Directed closeness scores

Ego	InCloseness	OutCloseness
Bob	40	24
Buddy	14.29	27.27
Mari	85.71	24
Martha	14.29	30
Phil	16.67	27.27
Sam	60	25
Sarah	54.55	24

Following the template given by Table 9.10, see if you can verify the directed betweenness scores for advice given in Table 9.11.

Mari definitely has the most control over the flow of advice in this network. Not only is she the expert to whom more of the others go for advice, but she also has key sources to get advice when she needs it perhaps to pass it on to those who come to her. We are not surprised by the lack of betweenness centrality for the pendants Buddy and Martha. How do you explain the zero scores for Bob and Sarah, who are otherwise part of the more active central group?

Tired of working it by hand? Several computer packages can perform the computations. See Hanneman and Riddle (2005) or Batagelj and Mrvar (2009).

9.2   Cutpoints and link pins

A useful means of assessing an individual point's social capital is to find the subgraphs of a graph both with and without the focal point. If the removal of the point increases or decreases the number of subgraphs, then that point is a cutpoint, an important bridge or link pin between otherwise unconnected subgroups. We have looked at two types of subgroups: components and cliques. Components represent nonredundant parts of a network, and so bridging components is a source of weak tie social capital. Cliques represent cohesive parts of a network; linking cliques can be a source of strong tie social capital.

With regard to components, if there are multiple components then there is an opportunity for a person to step in and become a bridge between components, which would span a structural hole, by definition, and give that person social capital. As HR managers, we would want to try to identify the person who might best serve such a role, and try to find ways to bring that person into contact with one or more members of the other component(s). To see if removing a person increases the number of

Table 9.10 Betweenness for directed data

Ego	Ordered pair of others	Intermediaries on geodesic(s)	Reverse ordered pair	Intermediaries on geodesic(s)	Proportion ego is on: order, reverse	Betweenness
Mari	Bob, Buddy	No geo	Buddy, Bob	Mari>Sam	0,1	
	Bob, Martha	No geo	Martha, Bob	Phil>Mari>Sam	0,1	
	Bob, Phil	No geo	Phil, Bob	Mari>Sam	0,1	
	Bob, Sam		Sam, Bob		0,0	
	Bob, Sarah	i. Mari	Sarah, Bob	Sam	0.5,0	
		ii. Sam				
	Buddy, Martha	No geo	Martha, Buddy	No geo	0,0	
	Buddy, Phil	No geo	Phil, Buddy	No geo	0,0	
	Buddy, Sam	Mari	Sam, Buddy	No geo	1,0	
	Buddy, Sarah	Mari	Sarah, Buddy	No geo	1,0	
	Martha, Phil		Phil, Martha	No geo	0,0	
	Martha, Sam	Phil>Mari	Sam, Martha	No geo	1,0	
	Martha, Sarah	Phil>Mari	Sarah, Martha	No geo	1,0	Sum=9.5
	Phil, Sam	Mari	Sam, Phil	No geo	1,0	9.5/30
	Phil, Sarah	Mari	Sarah, Phil	No geo	1,0	*100
	Sam, Sarah		Sarah, Sam	No geo	0,0	=31.67

139

Table 9.11   Betweenness scores

Ego	Betweenness	Normalized betweenness
Bob	0	0
Buddy	0	0
Mari	9.5	31.67
Martha	0	0
Phil	4	13.33
Sam	5.5	18.33
Sarah	0	0

Table 9.12   Subgraphs

Relation	Bicomponents	Cliques
Undirected communication	Sam, Sarah, Buddy, Phil, Mari Bob, Sam Phil, Martha	Sam, Mari, Sarah
Directed advice	Bob, Mari, Sam, Sarah Mari, Phil Buddy, Mari Martha, Phil	Bob, Mari, Sam Mari, Sam, Sarah

components, we look at the bicomponents. Points that appear in multiple bicomponents are cutpoints, serving to bridge what would otherwise be disjoint components.

With regard to cliques, once we have the cliques, clans, or k plexes identified, we can look to see if any individuals have multiple membership. If a person appears in multiple clique-like subgroups, then that person is embedded strongly in the structure and may be able to mobilize resources. If a person is the only common member in any pair of cliques, then that person may be an important linking pin and may be especially influential as a result.

Tabulating the bicomponents and cliques found for the communication and advice sociographs (in Chapter 8), examination of the graphs revealed the following. Table 9.12 shows that, in the communication network, Sam and Phil are weak tie bridges, while there are no strong tie pins if we restrict our attention to the strict definition of a 1 clique. Nevertheless,

Sam, Mari, and Sarah each gain some strong tie social capital as a result of their cohesion. Of course, we may find some strong tie pins if we loosen our definition of a clique, using 2 cliques or 2 plexes, for example. In such small groups, however, we are unlikely to gain many new insights.

In the advice network, we can see that Mari is a weak tie bridge joining three separate subgroups, while Phil weakly joins two nominal subgroups. Mari and Sam are both strong tie pins across cliques, but since they link the same cliques their social capital is less valuable to each than if either were the sole overlap. It is potentially more valuable to the organization, however.

9.3 Who's who

We return to the undergraduate cohort networks, this time to get egocentric measures for the students. With 89 students, we'll focus on the distribution of social capital. It is tempting to take the expeditious route using multiple centrality measures, but we cannot do so for this example. Why? Because the 'talk most' relation is defined as being directed. So we must run our three measures in turn.

Let's start with degree centrality. On average, students maintain about five others in their cohort among those they talk to most frequently, and each student has about five others in the cohort who likewise report talking most to them. Students named as few as zero and as many as 15 others and were named by from zero to as many as 16 others for this relation. The standard deviation reveals that the distribution falls mostly in the range from 0 to 10. An examination of the individual scores shows a triangular distribution, with most students naming just one or two others.

The closeness scores show a difference in how well members can reach others versus how well others can reach them. The mean InCloseness is about 7, suggesting that an average chain of seven intermediaries are

Descriptive statistics

		OutDegree	InDegree	Normalized OutDegree	Normalized InDegree
1	Mean	4.820	4.820	5.478	5.478
2	Standard deviation	2.874	3.008	3.266	3.418
8	Minimum	0.000	0.000	0.000	0.000
9	Maximum	15.000	16.000	17.045	18.182
10	No. of observations	89.000	89.000	89.000	89.000

		InFarness	OutFarness	InCloseness	OutCloseness
1	Mean	2752.685	2752.685	7.178	3.883
2	Standard deviation	2783.881	1552.137	3.986	1.564
8	Minimum	818.000	1042.000	1.124	1.124
9	Maximum	7832.000	7832.000	10.758	8.445
10	No. of observations	89.000	89.000	89.000	89.000

		Betweenness	Normalized betweenness
1	Mean	134.438	1.756
2	Standard deviation	207.748	2.714
8	Minimum	0.000	0.000
9	Maximum	1223.772	15.984
10	No. of observations	89.000	89.000

needed for any arbitrary student to reach any other student. In contrast, the OutCloseness paints a more cohesive picture of the structure, with students better positioned to access global information and resources from any arbitrary student.

The betweenness centrality distribution reveals a rather low mean, less than 2, with a standard deviation that is larger than the mean. For the most part, students have little control over the flows between others in the cohort. There are exceptions, however, indicated by the maximum score of almost 16. Control and opportunities for brokerage are concentrated in the network positions of just a few students.

9.4   Structural holes

We have so far dealt with *structural holes* as an important concept, capturing the critical essence of weak tie social capital. Analytically, we have described them only as ties that do not exist where they would be expected. This is a rather oversimplified definition. While it can be helpful in initially understanding the ideas of network diagnostics, a richer definition and more precise measures are needed for assessing social capital.

Burt (1992) defines *structural holes as the absence of redundancy, either by cohesion or by equivalence*. Redundancy by cohesion exists when a focal actor, ego, has ties to alters who are also directly tied to each other. That seems straightforward enough. You might simply ask whether my friends are friends of each other.

Redundancy exists by equivalence when, in the absence of such cohesion, ego has ties to alters who have other ties into the same subgroups. In the closest case, my friends are not friends, but they have other common friends besides me. Equivalence can, however, be further removed, as it might be that my friends are neither friends nor do they have other common friends, but each of them has friends who either are or have common friends. There may be any number of steps in the logical chain. In practice, of course, each step makes my friends a tad less equivalent, so that there is an underlying continuum to capture.

The measurement of structural holes tries to capture these ideas within an ego network. *By ego network, we mean the network among a focal ego's contacts, not counting ties to ego.* Burt (1992) has developed five related measures. Of these, constraint and effective size together best reflect the structural holes in ego's network. Constraint is an inverse measure, being directly related to redundancy. It is also a concentration index and so must be interpreted in conjunction with the overall or effective size of ego's network. Hierarchy then gauges the extent to which constraint is due to a single alter. Ego betweenness measures the extent to which ego has opportunities to broker among his or her contacts. Effective size and efficiency are components of constraint that help in the overall interpretation. Let's define how each is computed:

- *Effective size.* Burt's measure of the effective size of ego's network is essentially the number of alters minus the average degree of alters within the ego network, not counting ties to ego.
- *Efficiency.* The effective size divided by the number of alters in ego's network.
- *Constraint.* Burt's constraint measure is essentially a measure of the extent to which ego is invested in people who are invested in other of ego's alters. That is, it measures the extent to which ego's ties are concentrated in redundant contacts.
- *Hierarchy.* Burt's adjustment of constraint, indicating the extent to which constraint on ego is concentrated in a single alter.
- *Ego betweenness.* Our betweenness centrality measure applied only to pairs of alters among ego's direct contacts. This measure ignores pairs of others who are not among ego's direct contacts.

Let's look at the structural hole measures for advice relations in our board of directors.

To understand the computations, let's look at Mari. She has a degree of five, based on her direct ties. That is, we had previously counted her contacts and she has ties of either direction to five others in the group.

	Degree	Effective size	Efficiency	Constraint	Hierarchy	Ego betweenness
Bob	2.000	1.000	0.500	1.235	0.057	0.000
Buddy	1.000	1.000	1.000	1.000	1.000	0.000
Mari	5.000	4.000	0.800	0.517	0.260	6.500
Martha	1.000	1.000	1.000	1.000	1.000	0.000
Phil	2.000	2.000	1.000	0.500	0.000	1.000
Sam	3.000	2.000	0.667	0.751	0.057	2.500
Sarah	2.000	1.000	0.500	1.125	0.000	0.000

Ignoring ties to Mari, and only looking at ties among ego's contacts, one had ties to two others of these contacts, two of these contacts each have one tie to another of these contacts and the remaining two contacts do not have any ties to other contacts of Mari's. So the average degree among ego's alters in the ego network is $(2+1+1+0+0)/5 = .8$. Effective size is then ego's degree (5) less the average degree among ego's alters in the ego network (.8), resulting in 4 when rounded to an integer (since size must be in contacts). In other words, since Sam is tied to both Sarah and Bob, who are tied to Mari, Sam is redundant. Hence, the effective size is four. Efficiency is then 4 out of 5, or 80 percent.

Constraint is measured by taking a product of the proportion of ties ego has to each alter by the number of ties that alter has to other alters in ego's network, squaring the product and then summing over all of ego's contacts. A lower score indicates less constraint, and thus more structural holes in ego's network given the effective size.

Ego betweenness is the number of geodesics among pairs of ego's contacts that ego is on. This differs from our earlier measure of betweenness centrality in that we look at geodesics only among pairs of ego's contacts. For Mari as ego, pairs involving Martha are not counted. We can return to Table 9.10, adjusted accordingly in Table 9.13.

In this chapter, we covered methods for analyzing the social capital available to members based on their individual, or egocentric, positions in the social structure. When combined with the sociocentric methods and applied to properly obtained and processed network data, the egocentric measures give us a sense of who has how much social capital, of what type, and what they can do with it. Knowing this, we can more effectively manage networks to aid in the functioning of formal organizations.

Take some time to review the material in this part. Then we'll wrap up this book with a recap of what you should know before putting your new knowledge into practice.

Table 9.13 Computing ego betweenness

Ego	Ordered pair of others	Intermediaries on geodesic(s)	Reverse ordered pair	Intermediaries on geodesic(s)	Proportion ego is on: order, reverse	Betweenness
Mari	Bob, Buddy	No geo	Buddy, Bob	Mari>Sam	0,1	
	Bob, Phil	No geo	Phil, Bob	Mari>Sam	0,1	
	Bob, Sam		Sam, Bob		0,0	
	Bob, Sarah	Mari(Sam)	Sarah, Bob	Sam	0.5,0	
	Buddy, Phil	No geo	Phil, Buddy	No geo	0,0	
	Buddy, Sam	Mari	Sam, Buddy	No geo	1,0	
	Buddy, Sarah	Mari	Sarah, Buddy	No geo	1,0	
	Phil, Sam	Mari	Sam, Phil	No geo	1,0	
	Phil, Sarah	Mari	Sarah, Phil	No geo.	1,0	Sum=
	Sam, Sarah		Sarah, Sam		0,0	6.5

145

10 Social networks and social capital in action, revisited

We have now covered enough material to be able to conduct a meaningful social network analysis in a formal organization, putting both the methods and the concepts into practice. Let's review the 'knows' in doing a network analysis project.

10.1 Know the group or organization
The first thing you need to do is to introduce yourself to the group. Discuss why you are working with this group. Learn who the members are and ask them to describe each person's role in the group. Do they work closely as a team, or do they work independently of one another? Also describe the overall activities of the group. The group can be a work organization, such as a business or nonprofit, or a social organization, such as a fraternity, club, sports team, church, or any other well-defined group, such as students in a class. So it's important to really understand what they are trying to accomplish.

Keep in mind that you need to have access to the group and they must be willing to answer questions about their social relations, in terms of task-related activities such as communication, advice, and trust. They need to know about you, as well, in order to gain credibility.

You should also find out some things about the members themselves. Obtain some attribute and affiliation data on the members of the group. Consider attributes such as age, gender, ethnicity, education (highest level of schooling completed), tenure (how long they have been in the organization), and position. Affiliations to think about include where they are from or went to school, what community groups they support, or what hobbies they favor. Listen to what they have to say and choose attributes or affiliations accordingly.

Then just follow the chapter on gathering data carefully. You'll need to write a survey that gets at relevant types of social relations. As noted above, communication, advice, and trust are the default three, and these should be work related, rather than personal, but other types of relations might be important for the group at hand. Build on examples, from the text or others, but be sure to modify them for your group – make them as specific and as behavioral as possible, using language that is native to the group.

At this step, consider candidate questions to get at each type of relation needed. Make sure you can justify why you chose those items, how you altered them for your group to interpret them accurately, and the survey format you used.

Use the survey administration to learn as well. Be prepared to run into unexpected problems. How did you overcome them? Did everyone respond? If not, why not? If so, how did you ensure their responses? Discuss any general observations about the responses. Was there mostly agreement in reporting ties or did you find many instances where one person reported a tie to another who did not respond in kind? What did you make of such unrequited ties? Consider what the answers to these questions tell you about the group, the members, and the social relations.

10.2 Know the data

First follow the chapter on preparing data to construct adjacency matrices from your survey responses. You can do this directly in UCINET or you can do this in Excel and then import to UCINET. Also, prepare your attribute data accordingly, resulting in similarity or dissimilarity matrices.

Then analyze the sociocentric structure. You'll need to compute the network densities and identify any subgroups. As far as subgroups go, just look for components, bicomponents, and simple cliques. You'll also need to create a sociograph using the NetDraw software. Using attribute and affiliation data, see if any of your three social relations are more likely to occur if the members involved in the relation are similar or dissimilar on the attributes or share affiliations.

Next, analyze the egocentric position of each member. Here you'll need degree, closeness, and betweenness centrality for each member. Keep in mind that, for directed relations, you should get both InDegree and OutDegree, as well as both InCloseness and OutCloseness. You'll already have the information you need to see if any members are cutpoints from the analysis of sociocentric structure.

Present the networks. Provide the sociographs for each of the three networks: communication, trust, and advice. Describe the overall structure, comparing the three networks to each other as well as to the formal organizational chart. Do you observe any potentially problematic structures (such as bow ties, implosions, etc.)? Do they seem problematic for this group?

10.3 Know the people

Imagining that you are each member of the group, for each individual pull together their information across all networks. The objective here is to see who has social capital and what they can do with it. We assess the former by looking at our numbers:

- Centrality: the more centrality, the more social capital. Degree and closeness give access benefits; betweenness gives control benefits. Relate these to the material in Part I.
- Subgroups: membership in a clique provides some strong tie social capital, so we first look at the membership in cliques. If there are no cliques, then these numbers give rise to no new information about social capital beyond that captured in centrality. If cliques do exist, then members of the clique have strong ties to one another, and the potential social capital that comes from such strong ties.

If multiple cliques exist, then we can look for persons who are in more than one of the cliques. Overlapping cliques reinforce the cohesion and make those who link the cliques potential mobilizers and good change agents. How much social capital depends on whether that person is the only link between the cliques. If others are also in the same multiple cliques then the social capital is shared.

What can members do with strong tie social capital stemming from their inclusion in cliques? From their position as link pin of multiple cliques? How does that fit with your setting?

We can also ask whether a person is a bridge between nonequivalent subgroups by asking whether the number of components increases if we remove that person and their ties. If the removal of a person increases the number of components, then that person is bridging multiple components. In so doing, they are reaching nonequivalent parts of the network, and would have weak tie social capital, as this is a spanning of a structural hole. We check this by seeing who is in multiple bicomponents.

What use is weak tie social capital? Can it be used in that way in your group? If so, what will happen? If not, what prevents its use?

10.4   Know the social structure

Imagining that you are the director of human resources for this organization, for each network pull all the information together, across all individuals. The objective here is to describe the networks and compare the informal relations captured in the networks to the formal structure and work of the group. How much of a role does social capital play in this organization? How is it distributed?

Does each informal network reinforce the formal organization chart? Does the informal structure serve the organization? That is, consider the organization and its work and objectives. Are these served by social capital in general? By strong tie social capital? By weak tie social capital? Part I will help you apply your measures.

You can begin by considering the egocentric measures you just reported. Who has the most social capital? Given the group and their position in it, what can they do with this social capital? Is it a good thing that this person(s) has the most social capital? Why or why not?

Then you'll need the sociocentric measures. Each set of measures tells us something:

- *Densities.* If they work closely together as a team, then we would expect dense relations between them; if they work separately or in different locations, we would expect lower densities.
- *Transitivities.* If the organization relies on a unified group to compete against other collectives, then cohesion is important and we'd like to see higher transitivities. If innovation and within-group competition are keys to the group's strategy, then lower transitivities would indicate less redundancy. For example, consider what kind of social capital would be more useful for an organization attempting to change its strategy or structure versus one trying to become most efficient within a long-served market. Which describes your group better?
- *Centrality.* What is the distribution of positions in the informal structure? Is centrality concentrated or is the network more decentralized? How does this serve or hinder the organization's functioning? Are the most central individuals also those with the most formal authority or workflow interdependence? Do lower level or peripheral persons (in terms of organizational role) have the least centrality? Are there reasons why either pattern would be helpful or harmful?
- *Subgroups.* Do subgroups follow along departmental or 'chain of command' lines? Do subgroups implode, explode, or connect? Are structural holes apparent? Again, consider the theory, concepts, and applications we've covered and think about how subgroups can foster or hinder key types of activity for your organization. In particular, components and bicomponents help us see how much weak tie social capital the group has and how it is distributed. Cliques and clique-like subgroups tell us about strong tie social capital. Relate these to the theoretical material as applied in your setting. Does the distribution of social capital seem to undermine formal authority or does it actually enable people to get work done in spite of a poor formal structure? For example, a clique that cuts across levels, involving an owner, a supervisor, and an employee, might give rise

to favoritism or it might provide for rapid decision making – or both.

In addition to comparing each network to the formal structure, also compare the networks to each other. Does the trust network look like the communication network and the advice network? Do the different types of informal ties support or contradict each other?

10.5   Know the processes

You should also try to understand the formative basis of the networks. That is, conduct tests for homophily/heterophily. Can you identify factors that help to hold the informal structure together? If so, how can they be used either to correct problems or to capitalize on opportunities provided by the informal side of your organization and how it operates in conjunction with the formal work and objectives?

Form an overall diagnosis of whether the informal networks are operating to help this group accomplish its goals or to hinder them. Would you change the formal organization on the basis of the networks? Would you alter the informal relations? If you did have to alter informal relations, how would you do so? Are there any actions you think the organization could take to make the most out of the social capital of individuals? Should someone be promoted or given more responsibility? Less?

10.6   Know how to use what you know

After completing a project like this, you will have mastered both the basics and the nuances of social network analysis. You can take what you have learned into the workforce, in three ways:

- as an employee, to help you manage you own career;
- as a manager, to help you utilize the social capital in your organization;
- as a consultant, to help organizations diagnose problems and find solutions.

Appendix

Part I review

1. According to Krackhardt and Hanson (1993), mapping trust networks has proven most useful in diagnosing:
   a. low productivity;
   b. failing change efforts;
   c. routine conflicts;
   d. political conflicts.
2. Since the formal organization chart is designed for efficiency and accountability, if the informal network does not follow the formal chart it indicates a problem with the informal network.
   a. True.
   b. False.
3. According to Krackhardt and Hanson (1993), an imploded pattern occurs when:
   a. employees in a formal group relate only with members of other groups and not among themselves;
   b. employees in a formal group relate mostly among themselves, with few links to other groups;
   c. many employees are linked to a single person, but not to each other;
   d. there are no relationship ties between groups where you might otherwise expect them.
4. According to Krackhardt and Hanson (1993), to map the social network of a company, we personally observe the interactions among employees over a period of time.
   a. True.
   b. False.
5. Social relations require ongoing, frequent interaction between two parties.
   a. True.
   b. False.
6. A Social tie necessarily exists whenever a reporting relationship is shown in the organization chart.
   a. True.
   b. False.
7. According to Krackhardt and Hanson (1993), advice relations are those in which individuals exchange:

    a. political support;
    b. personal secrets;
    c. general information about the organization;
    d. task-specific information.

8. According to Coleman (1988), social capital is:
    a. a devestment;
    b. sometimes appropriable;
    c. entirely fungible;
    d. a private good;
    e. all of the above.

9. According to Granovetter (1973), which of the following types of ties best provides access to nonredundant information?
    a. best friend;
    b. weak;
    c. negative;
    d. strong;
    e. cohesive.

10. Appropriability refers to the transferring of a social relation from one type of activity or exchange to another type.
    a. True.
    b. False.

11. According to Granovetter (1973), for which of the following reasons can no strong tie be a bridge between nonredundant parts of a network?
    a. The process of homophily.
    b. The principle of affective imbalance.
    c. The low costs of maintaining strong ties.
    d. All of the above.
    e. None of the above.

12. According to Burt (2001), the echo hypothesis maintains that:
    a. information flow is enhanced with tie strength;
    b. information accuracy rises with tie strength;
    c. information flow is more two-way when ties are strong;
    d. a false sense of certainty is bred by strong ties.

13. According to Obstfeld (2005), joining two parties with incomplete resources can create value.
    a. True.
    b. False.

14. When you invest in building your social capital, you do so with a guarantee of future payback.
    a. True.
    b. False.

15. According to Coleman (1988), the extent to which norms will develop as a form of social capital depends on:
    a. the up-to-dateness of partners;
    b. the costs of information surveillance;
    c. the trustworthiness of the environment;
    d. all of the above;
    e. none of the above.
16. According to Obstfeld (2005), sustained iungens activity creates a social structure that is:
    a. more dense;
    b. more sparse;
    c. more replete in structural holes;
    d. all of the above;
    e. none of the above.
17. According to Burt (1997), which of the following is/are among the information-related benefits of social capital?
    a. Referrals.
    b. Control.
    c. Brokering.
18. According to Burt, the value of the information- and control-related benefits of social capital is contingent on characteristics of the formal organization.
    a. True.
    b. False.
19. Homophily describes:
    a. the process by which persons with social relations become dissimilar;
    b. the process by which similar persons form social relations;
    c. the process by which persons with similar ties gain similar benefits.
20. According to Burt (1997), social capital operates in which way with respect to human capital and economic capital?
    a. Multiplicatively.
    b. Independently.
    c. Logarithmically.
    d. Additively.
21. According to Coleman (1988), closure in a network facilitates trust because actors can:
    a. verify information using multiple sources;
    b. provide strong sanctions when norms are violated;
    c. maintain and act on reputations for obligations.
22. According to Coleman (1988), the three primary forms of social capital are:

     a. norms, obligations, and information channels;
     b. obligations, information channels, access;
     c. reciprocity, obligations, and expectations;
     d. norms, expectations, and obligations.

23.   According to Coleman (1988), closure in a network occurs when:
     a. those to whom ego is tied have no ties to the same other subgroups;
     b. those to whom ego is tied have multiple relations to ego;
     c. those to whom ego is tied have other ties to each other;
     d. those to whom ego is tied maintain ties only to ego.

24.   According to Reagans and his colleagues (2004), internal network density is detrimental to team performance.
     a. True.
     b. False.

25.   According to Marsden and Gorman (1999), which of the following is among the primary disadvantages of social capital methods of recruitment?
     a. Information quality.
     b. Strategic potential.
     c. Appearance of illegitimacy.
     d. Low costs.
     e. Efficiency.

26.   According to Fernandez and his colleagues (2001), which of the following are elements of the richer pool mechanism by which referrals for new hires might bring value to the hiring firm?
     a. Inferred homophily in human capital between referrer and applicant.
     b. Actual homophily in human capital between referrer and applicant.
     c. Negative homophily in human capital between referrer and applicant.
     d. All of the above.
     e. None of the above.

27.   Fernandez and his colleagues (2001) found that most of the value to firms of using referrals for new hires comes through their being significantly more qualified in terms of measurable job characteristics, thereby reducing post-hire training costs.
     a. True.
     b. False.

28.   According to Reagans and his colleagues (2004), which network measure reflects the weak tie social capital of work teams?
     a. Internal density.
     b. External density.
     c. External range.

29. According to Broschak (2004), the social capital generated by personal relations among exchange managers provides what value?
   a. Maximizes opportunism.
   b. Reduces coordination.
   c. Eases conflict resolution.
30. According to Marsden and Gorman (1999), which of the following recruitment methods is thought to be more desirable for a job with extensive on-the-job training?
   a. Direct contacts.
   b. Referrals.
   c. Job postings.
   d. Merit systems.
31. According to Brass and Labianca (1999), a negative tie is one that requires a lot of time and emotional involvement to maintain.
   a. True.
   b. False.
32. According to Brass and Labianca (1999), which of the following are reasons that negative social relations may have greater impact than positive social relations?
   a. Negative relations occur more frequently.
   b. Negative relations are more ambiguous.
   c. Negative relations cost more to maintain.
   d. All of the above.
   e. None of the above.
33. According to McGinn and Keros (2002), social interactions in the workplace can often be viewed as negotiations.
   a. True.
   b. False.
34. According to Koput and Gutek (in press), which kind of ties help to displace ascription.
   a. Strong cross-status ties.
   b. Weak same status ties.
   c. Strong same status ties.
   d. Weak cross-status ties.
35. According to McGinn and Keros (2002), which logic of exchange was successful among those with weaker ties?
   a. Mutualistic.
   b. Cooperative.
   c. Competitive.
   d. Malevolent.
   e. None of the above.

36. In the study by Mehra and his colleagues (2001), high self-monitors used their experience to tap into more weak tie social capital.
    a. True.
    b. False.
37. According to Higgins and Nohria (1999), which of the following best describes the downside of having a mentor provide access to information and resources too early in your career with a company?
    a. It may reduce your motivation to develop other ties.
    b. It may reduce others' motivation to develop ties to you.
    c. It may hinder your development of competence and self-efficacy.
    d. All of the above.
    e. None of the above.
38. According to Roth (2004), which of the following is the primary mechanism leading to tokenism?
    a. Bandwidth.
    b. Legitimation.
    c. Homophily preferences.
    d. Status expectations.
    e. None of the above.
39. According to McGinn and Keros (2002), which logic of exchange was promoted by stronger ties?
    a. Mutualistic.
    b. Cooperative.
    c. Competitive.
    d. Malevolent.
    e. None of the above.
40. According to Meyerson (1999), which type of ties lead to larger compensation at higher level managerial jobs?
    a. Weak.
    b. Strong.

Part II   review

1. To find out what behaviors indicate specific relations of interest in a particular group, we can do which of the following?
    a. Interview group members.
    b. Conduct a pilot survey of sample questions with a focus group.
    c. Observe the group at work.
    d. All of the above.
    e. None of the above.
2. What factors determine whether to treat a relation as directed or undirected?

    a. Which way the wind blows.
    b. Which is easier for data handling and analysis.
    c. How interaction is initiated in context.
    d. Whether other questions are directed or undirected.

3. A pilot survey to understand context is conducted by doing which of the following?
    a. Talking to subjects.
    b. Examining documents.
    c. Observing the group.
    d. Giving sample questions to a focus group.
    e. All of the above.

4. To establish content, the wording of survey questions should have what properties?
    a. Proper directionality.
    b. Attitudinal anchors.
    c. Bidirectionality.
    d. Behavioral anchors.
    e. Generality.
    f. Specificity.

5. Demographic variables are examples of:
    a. social ties;
    b. affiliations;
    c. attributes.

6. In directed relations, how is interaction initiated?
    a. By formally requiring two parties to exchange.
    b. As a byproduct of other interaction between two parties.
    c. By one party seeking out another for the relation.
    d. As a result of a third-party referral.

7. Attributes include:
    a. demographics, such as age, race, gender, ethnicity, and so forth;
    b. human capital, such as education and experience;
    c. personality traits and attitudes;
    d. all of the above;
    e. none of the above.

8. Which of the following describes observing the group to understand the context?
    a. Giving a pilot survey of sample questions to a focus group.
    b. Examining documents including the organization chart.
    c. Conducting structured interviews outside of the workplace.
    d. Taking notes while becoming an unintrusive part of the workplace.
    e. All of the above.

9. If interaction occurs when one party seeks out another, what is the directionality?
   a. Multidirected.
   b. Undirected.
   c. Directed.
   d. Non-directed.
   e. Bidirected.
10. In defining relational questions, we want to be as generic as possible.
    a. True.
    b. False.
11. Possible formats for a network survey include:
    a. hunt and peck;
    b. checklist;
    c. round robin;
    d. fill in the blanks;
    e. circle names.
12. If interaction occurs as a byproduct of other interaction, what is the directionality?
    a. Directed.
    b. Multidirected.
    c. Bidirected.
    d. Non-directed.
    e. Undirected.
13. Which of the following implies a behavioral anchor?
    a. Who would you go to if . . . ?
    b. Who have you gone to when . . . ?
    c. Who should you go to for . . . ?
14. The four principles for constructing a network survey are:
    a. content, communication, context, and cooperation;
    b. control, conduct, conversation, and coordination;
    c. content, context, confidentiality, and convenience;
    d. workflow, advice, and family;
    e. communication, trust, and advice.
15. To find out what language is used to capture specific relations of interest in a particular group, we can do which of the following?
    a. Interview group members.
    b. Conduct a pilot survey of sample questions with a focus group.
    c. Examine documents and records.
    d. All of the above.
    e. None of the above.
16. Specificity in wording content means doing which of the following?

    a. Using abstract concepts.
    b. Using generic terms.
    c. Using broad categories.
    d. None of the above.

17. In which type of adjacency matrix must entries be 0 or 1?
    a. Directed.
    b. Binary.
    c. Valued.
    d. Undirected.

18. A directed adjacency matrix is one in which entries can be any non-negative integer by definition.
    a. True.
    b. False.

19. Which responses are entered down the column labeled for the respondent in an adjacency matrix?
    a. Who the respondent goes to for a directed relation.
    b. Who comes to the respondent for a directed relation.
    c. Who shares an undirected relation with the respondent.

20. How are survey responses for who a person goes to entered into an adjacency matrix?
    a. Across rows.
    b. Down columns.
    c. Diagonally.

21. An adjacency matrix in which all entries must be 'either or' is called:
    a. binary;
    b. valued;
    c. undirected;
    d. directed.

22. The match rule converts individual data to dyadic similarities.
    a. True.
    b. False.

23. How does the Euclidean distance rule convert individual data to dyadic?
    a. Taking the absolute difference between node i and node j.
    b. Placing a 1 in cell (i,j) if node i and node j are in the same category.
    c. Transposing and multiplying the actor by variable matrix.
    d. Correlating node i's vectors of responses with node j's vector.
    e. Taking the squared difference between node i and node j, summing, and taking the square root.

24. Which of the following defines symmetric relations?
    a. Cell(i,j)=cell(j,i) for all i and j.
    b. Cell(i,j)>0 for all i,j.

    c. Cell(i,j)=0=cell(i,j) for both i and j.

    d. Cell(i,i)=0= for all i.

25. Entries that represent the presence or absence of a relation define which of the following types of adjacency matrices?

    a. Undirected.

    b. Binary.

    c. Valued.

    d. Directed.

26. Transposing and multiplying an actor by variable affiliation matrix produces which measure?

    a. Euclidean distance.

    b. Absolute difference.

    c. Count of co-occurrences.

    d. Exact match.

27. Which of the following is/are true of a directed adjacency matrix?

    a. Diagonal entries should equal 0.

    b. Cell (i,j) should equal cell (j,i).

28. How does the match rule convert individual data to dyadic?

    a. Placing a 1 in cell (i,j) if node i and node j are in the same category.

    b. Correlating node i's vectors of responses with node j's vector.

    c. Taking the squared difference between node i and node j, summing, and taking the square root.

    d. Transposing and multiplying the actor by variable matrix.

    e. Taking the absolute difference between node i and node j.

29. We can cross-check an undirected adjacency matrix by making sure the matrix is symmetric around the diagonal entries.

    a. True.

    b. False.

30. We can cross-check a directed adjacency matrix by making sure the matrix is symmetric around the diagonal entries.

    a. True.

    b. False.

31. The order of rows and columns in an adjacency matrix need not be the same.

    a. True.

    b. False.

32. When an undirected relation is reported inconsistently, the initial and symmetrized adjacency matrices sum to what value?

    a. 0.

    b. 1.

    c. 2.

33. When a network question is directed, we can cross-check by using what matrices?
    a. Goes to and comes to.
    b. Initial and symmetrized.
    c. Goes to and transpose.
    d. Initial and transpose.
34. A visualization in which persons are represented by points and relations between them are represented as lines is called which of the following?
    a. Spirograph.
    b. Structural hole.
    c. Sociograph.
    d. Network survey.
35. The distance between two nodes is found by:
    a. counting the number of lines in the shortest path between them;
    b. counting the number of intermediary nodes in the shortest path between them.
36. Which of the following is/are among the basic principles for constructing a sociograph?
    a. Persons with the most ties should be near the center of the graph.
    b. Persons adjacent to one another should be drawn in closer proximity than persons who are more distant.
    c. Pairs with more common partners should be drawn in closer proximity than pairs with fewer common partners.
37. Summing down columns of a directed adjacency matrix gives which of the following?
    a. Total undirected ties.
    b. Total bidirected ties.
    c. Total directed ties out.
    d. Total directed ties in.
38. A geodesic is a sequence of lines forming a connection between two nodes with what property?
    a. Fewest intermediary nodes.
    b. Fewest lines.
    c. Most lines.
    d. Most intermediary nodes.
39. In a sociograph, points represent relations between persons.
    a. True.
    b. False.
40. Among the basic principles for constructing a sociograph, points with the most ties should be near the edge of the graph.

  a. True.
  b. False.

Part III   review

  1. How many components are there in the directed trust network formed from the director survey responses ?
     a. 0.
     b. 1.
     c. 2.
     d. 3.
  2. Cliques are a potential source of fragmentation in a social structure.
     a. True.
     b. False.
  3. Which of the following indicate greater social capital in an informal network?
     a. More blocks.
     b. More cliques.
     c. More overlap.
     d. More components and bicomponents.
  4. The density of a graph is the number of points that are included in any lines, divided by the total number of points.
     a. True.
     b. False.
  5. If the coefficient on a similarity matrix is positive and significant in a QAP regression, this is evidence for which process?
     a. Heterophily.
     b. Homophily.
     c. Strength of weak ties.
  6. What do we look for to see whether cliques bring cohesion to the organization?
     a. Overlap with other cliques.
     b. Agreement of cliques with formal structure.
     c. Overlap of cliques with components.
  7. Evidence for homophily would be found if a QAP regression output indicated which of the following?
     a. Negative coefficient on similarity matrix.
     b. Negative coefficient on dissimilarity matrix.
     c. Positive coefficient on dissimilarity matrix.
     d. Positive coefficient on similarity matrix.
  8. If every member of a network can reach every other member through a path of some length, which of the following must be true?

a. There are no cliques.
b. There are no bicomponents.
c. There is one transition.
d. There is one component.

9. According to Watts (1999), which of the following has a small clustering coefficient and high characteristic path length?
a. Small world.
b. Regular graph.
c. Connected cavemen.
d. He didn't say.
e. Random graph.

10. What do we look at for a sense of weak tie social capital available in a structure?
a. Cliques.
b. Bicomponents.
c. Components.

11. In the director trust network, which type of social capital does the structure provide more potential for developing?
a. Weak tie.
b. Strong tie.
c. Negative tie.
d. None of the above.

12. Which of the following indicate greater cohesion in a graph?
a. More blocks.
b. More cliques.
c. More overlap.
d. More components and bicomponents.

13. What is the fewest number of nodes in a bicomponent?
a. None.
b. One.
c. Two.
d. N.
e. N/2.

14. Which of the following assumptions of ordinary regression analysis is violated when using dyadic data to test for homophily in a social network?
a. Independence of observations.
b. Normality.
c. Linearity.
d. Homoskedasticity.

15. If there is a significant positive coefficient on a dissimilarity matrix in a QAP regression, which process is supported by the data?

     a. Equivalence.

     b. Heterophily.

     c. Homophily.

16.   A node with no ties in a network is called what?

     a. Pendant.

     b. Medallion.

     c. Zero pole.

     d. Isolate.

17.   How many cliques are there in the director trust network?

     a. 0.

     b. 1.

     c. 2.

     d. 3.

     e. 4.

18.   Cliques are a potential source of cohesion in a social structure.

     a. True.

     b. False.

19.   According to Watts (1999), the average distance between any two nodes is known as:

     a. clustering coefficient;

     b. characteristic path length.

20.   A sparse bicomponent structure suggests a deficiency in which of the following?

     a. Strong tie cohesion.

     b. Weak tie bridging.

     c. Strong tie bridging.

     d. Weak tie cohesion.

21.   A node with just one connection into a component is referred to as what?

     a. Isolate.

     b. Medallion.

     c. Unipole.

     d. Pendant.

22.   A subgraph is any collection of points selected from the whole graph.

     a. True.

     b. False.

23.   If someone is in more than one bicomponent, which of the following must be true?

     a. They are a pendant.

     b. They are a bridge.

     c. They are central.

     d. They are in at least two cliques.

24. What is the degree score for a pendant in an undirected graph?
    a. 0.
    b. 1.
    c. N−1.
    d. N.
    e. None of the above.
25. What is the betweenness score for an isolate?
    a. 0.
    b. N(N−1).
    c. .5.
    d. 100.
    e. N.
26. How is InDegree computed from a directed adjacency matrix?
    a. Row sum times column sum.
    b. Summing down column.
    c. Product across row.
    d. Summing across row.
    e. Product of diagonal.
27. According to Burt (1992), structural holes are defined by the absence of:
    a. redundancy by cohesion;
    b. redundancy by equivalence;
    c. both of the above;
    d. neither of the above.
28. Sarah is a cutpoint in the director trust network.
    a. True.
    b. False.
29. For the director trust network, Sarah is more trusted globally than is Mari.
    a. True.
    b. False.
30. Betweenness centrality captures what aspect of points in a graph?
    a. Global access.
    b. Control over flow.
    c. Local activity.
31. Closenesss centrality is defined as the average distance between a point and all other points.
    a. True.
    b. False.
32. What is the betweenness score for a pendant?
    a. 0.5.
    b. 1.

    c. 0.

    d. N(N−1)/2.

33. Which has a higher betweenness centrality?

    a. Pendant.

    b. Isolate.

    c. Neither.

34. Which measure of centrality best captures the ability of each person to quickly access others globally throughout a network?

    a. Betweenness.

    b. Density.

    c. Degree.

    d. Closeness.

    e. Transitivity.

35. According to Burt (1992), redundancy exists by equivalence when:

    a. ego's alters have ties to each other;

    b. there is an absence of cohesion;

    c. ego's alters have other ties into the same subgroups.

36. In the director communication network, Sarah's removal would increase the number of cliques.

    a. True.

    b. False.

37. Which measure(s) of individual position best capture(s) ability to mobilize the resources in a network toward a common objective?

    a. Bicomponent co-membership.

    b. Clique co-membership.

    c. Closeness centrality.

    d. Degree centrality.

    e. Betweenness centrality.

38. Which measure of centrality is defined in terms of intermediaries on geodesics connecting pairs of points?

    a. Cliqueness.

    b. Betweenness.

    c. Closeness.

    d. Degree.

39. According to Burt (1992), effective size is measured as:

    a. the extent to which ego's ties are concentrated in redundant contacts;

    b. the effective size divided by the number of alters in ego's network;

    c. betweenness centrality measure applied only to pairs of alters among ego's direct contacts;

    d. the number of alters minus the average degree of alters within the ego network, not counting ties to ego;

e. the extent to which constraint on ego is concentrated in a single alter.
40. According to Burt (1992), weak tie social capital is indicated by:
    a. high effective size, high constraint, high ego betweenness;
    b. high effective size, high constraint, low ego betweenness;
    c. low effective size, low constraint, low ego betweenness;
    d. high effective size, low constraint, low ego betweenness;
    e. high effective size, low constraint, high ego betweenness.

References

Arnold, B. and F. Kay (1999), 'Social capital, violations of trust, and the vulnerability of isolates', in S.M. Gabbay and R. Leenders (eds), *Corporate Social Capital and Liability*, Boston, MA: Kluwer Academic Press.

Baker, W. and R. Faulkner (1993), 'The social organization of conspiracy: illegal networks in the heavy electrical equipment industry', *American Sociological Review*, **58** (6), 837–60.

Batagelj, V. and A. Mrvar (2009), 'Pajek: program for analysis and visualization of large networks reference manual', http://vlado.fmf.uni lj.si/pub/networks/pajek/doc/pajekman.pdf.

Brass, D. (1984), 'Being in the right place: a structural analysis of individual influence in an organization', *Administrative Science Quarterly*, **29** (4) , 518–39.

Brass, D. and G. Labianca (1999), 'Social and social liabilities', in S.M. Gabbay and R. Leenders (eds), *Corporate Social Capital and Liability*, Boston, MA: Kluwer Academic Press.

Broschak, J. (2004), 'Managers' mobility and market interface: the effect of managers' career mobility on the dissolution of market ties', *Administrative Science Quarterly*, **49** (4), 608–40.

Burt, R.S. (1992), *Structural Holes: The Social Structure of Competition*, Cambridge, MA: Harvard University Press.

Burt, R.S. (1997), 'The contingent value of social capital', *Administrative Science Quarterly*, **42**, 339–65.

Burt, R.S. (2000), 'The network structure of social capital', in B.M. Staw and R. Sutton (eds), *Research in Organizational Behavior*, vol. 22, New York: Elsevier Science.

Burt, R.S. (2001), 'Bandwidth and echo: trust, information and gossip in social networks', in A. Cassella and J. Rausch (eds), *Networks and Markets: Contributions from Economics and Sociology*, New York: Russell Sage.

Coleman, J. (1988), 'Social capital in the creation of human capital', *American Journal of Sociology*, **94**, Supplement, S95–S120.

Fernandez, R., E.J. Castilla, and P. Moore (2001), 'Social capital at work: networks and employment at a phone center', *American Journal of Sociology*, **105** (55), 1288–1356.

Flap, H. and E. Boxman (1999), 'Getting a job as a manager', in S.M. Gabbay and R. Leenders (eds), *Corporate Social Capital and Liability*, Boston, MA: Kluwer Academic Press.

Granovetter, M. (1973), 'The strength of weak ties', *American Journal of Sociology*, **78** (6), 1360–80.

Hanneman, Robert A. and Mark Riddle (2005), *Introduction to Social Network Methods*, Riverside, CA: University of California, Riverside (published in digital form at http://faculty.ucr.edu/~hanneman/).

Higgins, M. and N. Nohria (1999), 'The sidekick effect', in S.M. Gabbay and R. Leenders (eds), *Corporate Social Capital and Liability*, Boston, MA: Kluwer Academic Press.

Koput, K.W. and B.A. Gutek (in press), *Gender Stratification in the IT Industry: Leaky Pipes and Cracked Prisms*.

Krackhardt, D. and J. Hanson (1993), 'Informal networks: the company behind the chart', *Harvard Business Review*, **71** (4), July/August, 104–11.

Marsden, P.V. and E.H. Gorman (1999), 'Social capital in internal staffing practices', in S.M. Gabbay and R. Leenders (eds), *Corporate Social Capital and Liability*, Boston, MA: Kluwer Academic Press, 180–96.

McGinn, K. and A. Keros (2002), 'Improvisation and the logic of exchange in socially embedded transactions', *Administrative Science Quarterly*, **47** (3) , 442–73.

Mehra, A., M. Kilduff, and D.J. Brass (2001), 'The social networks of high and low self monitors: implications for workplace performance', *Administrative Science Quarterly*, **46** (1), 121–46.

Meyerson, E. (1999) 'Social capital and social resources management', in S.M. Gabbay and R. Leenders (eds), *Corporate Social Capital and Liability*, Boston, MA: Kluwer Academic Press.

Obstfeld, D. (2005), 'Social networks, the tertius iungens orientation, and involvement in innovation', *Administrative Science Quarterly*, **50**, 100–130.

Reagans, R.E., E.W. Zuckerman, and B. McEvily (2004), 'How to make the team: social networks vs. demography as criteria for designing effective projects in a contract R&D firm', *Administrative Science Quarterly*, **49**, 101–33.

Roth, L. (2004), 'The social psychology of tokenism: status and homophily processes on Wall Street', *Sociological Perspectives*, **47** (2), 189–214.

Watts, D. (1999), *Small Worlds*, Princeton, NJ: Princeton University Press.

Index